ESSENTIAL WORDS FOR THE

Second Edition

GED

High School Equivalency Exam

Sydney L. Langosch, M.A.

D1500076

BARRON'S

DEDICATION

For my husband, Ken, and our family

ACKNOWLEDGMENTS

My thanks to the athletes who, in an earlier edition, allowed me to quote them, and the members of the GED Testing Service, the Center for Adult Learning and Educational Credentials, the American Council on Education for their guidance, and to the editors at Barron's Educational Series, Inc., who put forth that extra effort throughout the writing, editorial, and production processes of this book. My appreciation also for the support of my colleagues at Lado International College, Silver Spring Center, Silver Spring, Maryland.

Copyright © 2004, 1999 by Barron's Educational Series, Inc.

All inquiries should be addressed to:
Barron's Educational Series, Inc.
250 Wireless Boulevard
Hauppauge, NY 11788
http://www.barronseduc.com

Library of Congress Catalog Card No. 2003068840

ISBN-13: 978-0-7641-2357-3
ISBN-10: 0-7641-2357-2

Library of Congress Cataloging-in-Publication Data

Langosch, Sydney L.
   Essential words for the GED / by Sydney L. Langosch—2nd ed.
      p. cm.
   Includes bibliographical references (p.).
   ISBN 0-7641-2357-2 (alk. paper)
    1. Vocabulary tests—Study guides. 2. General educational development tests—Study guides. I. Title.

   PE1449.L29 2004
   428.1'076—dc22

                             2003068840

PRINTED IN THE UNITED STATES OF AMERICA
9 8 7 6 5 4 3

CONTENTS

INTRODUCTION

HOW TO USE THIS BOOK

In order to use *Essential Words for the GED, 2nd Edition* effectively to help you maximize your word power and to pass the GED, you must first determine how good your present vocabulary is. In Chapter 1 you will learn about vocabulary skills and how to use these skills to get the highest possible score on the five tests.

In Chapter 2 you have the opportunity to check your fluency and vocabulary skills through a few simple tests. Chapter 3 focuses on identifying your passive vocabulary. By turning those passive words into active ones, you will learn to read with greater accuracy, to cover test materials with better comprehension, and to write more proficiently. Chapter 4 will help you understand suffixes and prefixes so that you can build on base words that you already know.

Although GED tests do not include a spelling or vocabulary test area, these skills have a strong impact on all of the tests, especially on the Language Arts Writing Part 1 and Part 2. Chapter 5 provides useful spelling tips, and Chapter 6 heightens your awareness of special words such as modal auxiliaries *could* or *may* and many more.

Part Two of *Essential Words for the GED, 2nd Edition* consists of a list of more than 400 alphabetically arranged words that have been selected according to the frequency with which they appear in the GED practice tests, as well as recent television broadcasts and print media.

Appendix A consists of a special chart arranged according to subject area. The eight targeted areas for these words are social studies, graphs, mathematics, interpreting literature and the arts, writing skills, grammar, direction words, and science.

For those of you who want additional practice, Appendix B provides several more practice exercises based on words taken directly from the GED.

Strategies for Using This Book

- Set a schedule for yourself.

- Select 15 words a day on which to concentrate.

- Review the words in context from the different test areas.

- Review the spelling of the words.

- Begin a word list of your own.

- Carry a vocabulary notebook with you as faithfully as you carry your car keys or your bus tokens.

- Do not let one day go by without targeting words for study.

In about four weeks you will have reviewed familiar words or learned new words that are essential to your success in taking and completing the five GED tests.

Using a Dictionary

In order to get the most from *Essential Words for the GED, 2nd Edition*, use it along with a dictionary and refer to it every day. Not all words you may want to study are used exclusively in testing. An educated vocabulary also consists of words used by teachers, doctors, lawyers, businessmen, and other professionals.

Parts of Speech

For each entry you will discover whether the word is a noun, pronoun, verb, or adjective. Each main entry is then followed by a sample sentence.

Special Notes

There are special usage notes as well as spelling and grammar tips throughout the word list, giving added information for the study of the words in general.

PART ONE

CHAPTER 1

HOW *ESSENTIAL WORDS FOR THE GED* CAN HELP YOU

An important key to self-confidence is preparation.
— Arthur Ashe
The late World and U.S.
Championship tennis player

Studying for the Tests of General Educational Development (GED) is a lot like preparing for an important sports event: Just as you plan, practice, and work hard to improve your game, no matter which sport it is, you must get ready to take the GED with the same intensity.

Part of your preparation for the GED tests includes improving your vocabulary skills. Having a strong vocabulary will increase your ability to follow directions, choose the right words in your writing, and hone your reading skills. What's more, your mastery of the different content areas such as science, writing skills, mathematics, social studies, and literature and the arts, depends upon building a strong vocabulary that will add to your ability to communicate clearly in all walks of life.

TYPES OF QUESTIONS

A successful score on the five tests for the GED depends on the test taker's ability to write, speak, and hold a conversation about many subjects. Although there are no special vocabulary questions included in the GED tests, it is important to strengthen your vocabulary skills. Through a special effort to increase your vocabulary and review words you already know, you can assure yourself of achieving the best score possible on your GED test results.

In *Essential Words for the GED, 2nd Edition,* more than 400 words have been selected from several practice GED tests, as well as other sources, such as books, newspapers, the media, and technical publications. These targeted words will assist you in responding to the five types of tests.

Language Arts Writing Test (Part 1)

This part consists of 50 multiple-choice questions designed to measure your ability to use standard written English clearly and effectively.

The content areas of Part 1 may evaluate the following: the organization of your writing; correct sentence structure; grammar usage; and the mechanics of your writing style, such as correct capitalization, punctuation, and spelling, especially with regard to possessives, contractions, and homonyms.

This is an example of a type of question from Language Arts Writing Test (Part 1) that is designed to measure your ability to use standard written English clearly and effectively.

Q and A: Select the sentence that has correct capitalization and no punctuation errors.

    (A) In conclusion I promise you this: we will make greater advances in Productivity this year than in the past five year's combined.

    (B) In conclusion. I promise you this. We will make greater advances in productivity this year than in the past five years combined.

(C) In conclusion I promise you this: We will make greater advances in productivity this year than in the past five years combined.

The correct answer is (C) because the colon is followed by a capital letter when the content is more than a word or two.

Language Arts Writing Test (Part 2)

This part provides an expository topic on which you are required to write an original essay in which you present your opinion or explain your views about that topic. You will be evaluated on the clarity and organization of your paragraph, but you also must display an understanding of the elements of standard English, such as sentence structure and the parts of speech. You should be able to recognize sentence fragments and should avoid using these in your own essay. Understanding how to use the major parts of speech such as nouns, pronouns, verbs, adjectives, and adverbs is important for handling these questions successfully.

Each of the entries for words listed in Part Two of *Essential Words for the GED, 2nd Edition* includes a note on sentence parts, such as subject, verb, adjective, and adverb. (Also refer to pages 28–29 for precise definitions of these terms.)

Q and A: The following essay question illustrates what an individual might encounter on a Language Arts Writing Test for the GED:

The Pathfinder and the *Deer Slayer* by James Fenimore Cooper are early American short stories published in the eighteenth century. Describe characteristics of early eighteenth-century life, the settlers' habits, their background, and their interests and goals in beginning anew.

Social Studies

This portion of the GED contains 50 multiple-choice questions that measure the test taker's understanding of general concepts as well as specific issues related to U.S. history, world history, geography, civics and government, and economics.

Q and A: The following multiple-choice question illustrates what an individual might encounter on a GED test for Social Studies:

The collapse of the Soviet Union (Union of Soviet Socialist Republics) in the early 1990s led to an uncertainty about the country's future economic and political stability. One of the more noticeable effects was the steady decline in:

    (A) trade with South Africa

    (B) quality of health care

    (C) the birthrate

The answer for this multiple-choice question is (C) birthrate.

Science

This section presents the test taker 50 multiple-choice questions from the following content areas:

- Physical Science (35 percent)
- Life Science (45 percent)
- Earth and Space Science (20 percent)

Q and A: In science questions, the test taker is asked to demonstrate, analyze, and solve problems; explain results; interpret findings; and predict outcomes by selecting the correct multiple-choice answer.

Which of the following is an organ of the human body?

    (A) pupil

    (B) Golgi apparatus

    (C) organelle

    (D) brain

The correct answer in this case is (D), brain. None of the other choices offered is an example of an organ.

Language Arts Reading

This portion of the test is made up of 40 multiple-choice questions based on excerpts from literature, art, the media, and newspaper articles. An excerpt of the reading may include a selection of writing that is at least 200 to 400 words. A purpose question is presented to help you focus, but you are not asked to answer the question.

Q and A: The following multiple-choice question is an example of what an individual might encounter on the Language Arts Reading portion of the GED:

Keep these rules in mind: Throughout your employment period, be vigilant about potential conflicts of interest. Do not use your position with this company to obtain a personal benefit of any kind. Be sure to avoid any action or relationship that creates an appearance of a conflict of interest.

Q and A: Select a set of three words that illustrate the serious nature of this fictitious notice to employees.

(A) employment, period, any

(B) throughout, company, kind

(C) vigilant, conflict, avoid

The correct answer is (C) vigilant, conflict, avoid.

Mathematics

This section of the GED is divided into two parts, each with 25 questions. The questions on both parts are intended to measure general math skills and problem-solving ability. A Casio FX-250 calculator will be provided for you at the official GED Testing Center for use with Part One of the Mathematics portion. You will not be permitted to use your own calculator. A page of math formulas will also be provided to use as a reference.

The following four major areas are tested in the Mathematics portion.

(1) Number operations and number sense (20 to 30 percent)

(2) Measurement and geometry (20 to 30 percent)

(3) Data analysis, statistics, and probability (20 to 30 percent)

(4) Algebra, functions and patterns (20 to 30 percent)

Part One and Part Two have multiple-choice, standard grid, and coordinate plane grid questions.

The following is a sample of an alternate-formula question:

Q and A: A painter mixes many gallons of paint in a large cylindrical bucket so that there will be no difference in color among individual gallons. If 1 gallon of paint has a volume of approximately 8,000 cubic cm, what is the maximum number of whole gallons of paint that can be poured into the bucket?

(A) 3

(B) 7

(C) 9

(D) 11

(E) 37

The answer is (C) 9, because 10 whole gallons would not fit.

THE ESL (ENGLISH AS A SECOND LANGUAGE) READING COMPREHENSION

These questions test the skills for functional reading needed to cope with daily life encounters, such as giving and taking directions, interviewing, obtaining Internet information, and many other daily reading tasks. To learn more about these ESL questions, contact the American Council on Education, One Dupont Circle, Washington, DC 20036.

Comprehensive Questions

These types of questions require that the test taker interpret the intent of the question:

- To restate information accurately
- To summarize
- To arrange knowledge in its order of importance
- To state answers in chronological order
- To restate knowledge in new contexts
- To make intelligent guesses
- To draw conclusions by evaluating and using the information at hand

Application Questions

These types of questions require the test taker to use previous knowledge to solve problems by applying thinking processes to analyze and arrange information in new contexts.

Analysis Questions

Successful responses to these questions call on the test taker to explore and relate material to ideas.

BUILDING AN EFFECTIVE AND ACCURATE VOCABULARY

Although there is no designated vocabulary test for the GED, your responses to each part of the test will be enhanced by correct and accurate vocabulary skills. The following guidelines will assist you as you take the test, enhancing every written response.

1. Write the new word on a 4×5 index card.
2. Break it down into syllables.
3. Target words in your reading and in your conversations.

4. Say the word aloud, over and over.

5. Write it in the air.

6. Close your eyes and think that word. Imagine someone acting it out.

7. Bring to that word all of your sensory equipment. Can you smell it? See it? Hear it?

8. Check the meaning of the word in a reliable dictionary.

9. Use the word in a sentence. For this you can now turn your index card over and record your sentence on the opposite side.

10. Continue to study new words even after you have taken the test. Building your word power could become habit-forming.

Analyze the Word

In order to analyze a word such as *devalue*, make a few educated guesses. How many syllables? One or two? Then write this word on an index card. Use one side of the card at this point, but when you do record it, include hyphens (*de-val-ue*) to indicate how many syllables it has. Next, look for any prefixes or suffixes. You may ascertain that *de* is a prefix and you are correct. (More about prefixes and suffixes in Chapter 4.)

Pronunciation Guideline

One way to find out how to pronounce a word is to ask. Do not hesitate to ask someone to repeat the word. The stress of words is extremely important and often complicated. If you study the word *de-value*, you can see that the prefix *de* is a long *e* sound, as in *keep*. This prefix means to move away. Now say it aloud: *de-value*. Did you give the second syllable the hardest stress? Then you are well along in pronouncing that word.

Other Tips for Word Study

The order of the word list in *Essential Words for the GED, 2nd Edition* is alphabetical. It also includes usage, spelling, and grammar tips. The more you know about each word you study, the better you will be prepared for taking the five GED tests.

PRACTICE EXERCISE

This exercise will give you warm-up practice in word study.

Thinking of groups of words that are related is an efficient way to build your vocabulary skills. For Exercise 1, think of words that describe people. And since you know yourself better than anyone else, take two minutes (you can time yourself) to think about words that describe *you.*

Next, you can compare your word list with the one we thought of. Ours does not necessarily describe any one person. The left column contains words that describe. Try filling in the blank on the right with the correct letter for matching the definition.

1. *energetic* ____   a. *unusual*
2. *kinetic* ____   b. *full of energy*
3. *martyr* ____   c. *famous*
4. *tenacious* ____   d. *undecided*
5. *vapid* ____   e. *religious*
6. *ambivalent* ____   f. *boring*
7. *novel* ____   g. *unrelenting*
8. *eminent* ____   h. *active*
9. *pious* ____   i. *eager*
10. *zealous* ____   j. *saintlike*

Answers:

1. b	6. d
2. h	7. a
3. j	8. c
4. g	9. e
5. f	10. i

CHAPTER 2

EVALUATING YOUR WORD POWER

Nothing good comes in life or athletics unless a lot of hard work has preceded the effort.

— Roger Staubach
former NFL sports broad-caster and NFL quarterback

CHECK YOUR VOCAL CRUTCHES

The first step in evaluating your present vocabulary is to become aware of your pauses while you search for a word. How many times in your conversation do you unconsciously cover your lack of fluency with "you know," "get it?" "ummm?"

These and other devices for filling spaces without meaningful words are called vocal crutches. Actually, we all have a vocal crutch or two. These crutches help us to think ahead, but they also indicate a certain lack of fluency. If you use more than three or four of these a minute, you may not be as fluent as you wish to be.

It is possible to check this by listening to yourself. Every time you are on the phone, place a check mark on a piece of paper to give yourself an idea of what you said, then note the length of time of the phone call. Three minutes, nine vocal crutches. Not bad. But if you have three minutes with fifteen or twenty vocal crutches, then you need to reflect on your fluency.

TEST YOUR GED WORD POWER

A second way to evaluate your vocabulary is to complete the following tests. The words in these five exercises could be found on one of the five areas of the GED. In order to get a rough idea of what your vocabulary is, particularly as it relates to studying for the GED test, complete the following five tests. You do not need to time each test, but all of them should not take more than an hour.

Cover the answers that follow each test with your paper; however, do not begin to check any of the answers until you have completed all tests. When you do finish, uncover the answers, check yours against them, and total your score. Each correct answer in the evaluation is worth four points. Do not subtract for wrong answers. Do not give any one answer more points than another.

Test A

This exercise tests your power of recall. Examine the following column of five words. On the right side there is a column with a letter and a blank. Try to complete each blank with a word beginning with the letter that means the same as the word in the left column. Each correct answer is worth four points. The highest score possible is 20.

Example: severe   <u>harsh</u>

1. harmless   b _____

2. all-knowing   o _____

3. selfish   e _____

4. parts   c _____

5. 1,000 years   m _____

Answers: 1. benign   3. egocentric   5. millennium
              2. omniscient   4. composites

Test B

The next test is designed to check your knowledge of synonyms.
(A synonym is a word that has the same meaning as another
word.) Choose the best synonym for the numbered word.

Example: incognito

(Circle the correct answer.)

A. rare

B. unknown

C. famous

The correct answer is B.

Now try the following exercise based on the above example:

1. square

    A. having four equal sides

    B. having three equal sides

    C. having none of the above

2. alloy

    A. metal

    B. optics

    C. mixture

3. junket

    A. contract

    B. trip

    C. entertainment

4. scare

    A. frighten

    B. transfer

    C. reassure

5. urbane

    A. polished

    B. citified

    C. exaggerated

Answers: 1. A   2. C   3. B   4. A   5. A

Test C

The following exercises test your word recognition. Choose from the ten words below to complete these sentences. You will need five words.

abdicate	cynic	ecology	gratify	notorious
pristine	rustic	scrutinize	ultra	harness

1. When a king resigns from his throne, he is said to _____.

2. You may assume that everyone is a _____, but it is possible that you think that because you had a bad experience.

3. My family is looking for a _____ vacation spot for next summer.

4. The teacher will _____ every composition for mistakes in spelling and grammar.

5. If California could _____ more water power, it would be the garden spot of the United States.

Answers: 1. abdicate   4. scrutinize
              2. cynic   5. harness
              3. rustic

Test D

Now you need to think in reverse. Respond to the following words by writing the <u>opposite</u> meanings in the column on the right. The first and last letters will help you find the correct answer.

1. ancient   y_____g

2. square   r_____d

3. pristine   d_____d

4. wistful   h_____y

5. hearsay   p_____n

Answers: 1. young   4. happy
              2. round   5. proven
              3. damaged

Test E

Choose a sentence that gives a similar meaning to the first one stated, noting the underlined word.

1. The librarian's constant <u>monologue</u> about being quiet was more disruptive than the readers' conversation.

   A. The librarian talked without interruption.

   B. The librarian meant to be understanding.

   C. None of the readers was aware of the librarian.

2. Whenever Maria's friend is <u>solvent</u>, he takes her out to dinner.

   A. If Maria's friend is in a good mood, he takes her out to dinner.

   B. When he's late for a date, he takes her out to dinner.

   C. If Maria's friend has enough money, he takes her out to dinner.

3. The veterans' group is in <u>accord</u> about their plan to distribute the toys for needy children next week.

   A. The veterans are in agreement about the toys they will deliver next week.

   B. The veterans cannot decide how to give the needy children toys.

   C. The veterans are going to let the children's families pick out the toys.

4. When the supervisor deals with conflict at work, she prefers to avoid a <u>confrontation</u>.

   A. The supervisor does not like to meet conflicts head-on.

   B. The supervisor always refers the problem to her boss.

   C. The supervisor discusses the problem with the two parties involved.

5. My young nephew has a habit of <u>harassing</u> his parents until he gets what he wants.

   A. My nephew annoys his parents until he gets his way.

   B. My nephew always understands when his parents cannot give him what he wants.

   C. My nephew is an only child who always gets what he wants.

Answers: 1. A   2. C   3. A   4. A   5. A

To score the preceding five tests, give yourself four points for each correct answer in each test, then add them to find your score. The following will give you an idea of how you did.

Test	Points
A	
B	
C	
D	
E	
Total	

70–80	Good
80–90	Very Good
90–95	Excellent
95–100	**Exceptional**

CHAPTER 3

ACTIVATE YOUR PASSIVE VOCABULARY

Pressure makes a person more focused . . .

— Nancy Lopez
Ladies Professional Golf Association (LPGA) Hall of Famer, Winner of 48 LPGA tournaments including 3 major championships

WHAT *IS* A PASSIVE VOCABULARY?

We comprehend many more words than we actually use. Although we may understand up to 15,000 words, we use only about 75 or 80 percent of them. *Passive* and *active* are special terms used for distinguishing between those words we know and those that we actually use. For example, we may *understand* the word *hone*, which means to sharpen or to polish the quality of something, yet we may never say it or write it. Chances are we do not even know how to pronounce the word *hone*. We may have a vague idea of the meaning of the word and hesitate to use it. Does this count toward our vocabulary? Yes, most certainly, but it is only a part of our *passive* vocabulary.

Value of the Passive Vocabulary

We do not mean to imply that all of those words in our passive vocabulary are not useful. Becoming an expert communicator is greatly influenced by a strong passive vocabulary. Actually, selecting big words where simpler words will do is not always the most effective way to communicate. In fact, legal firms and other businesses are encouraging less pretentious and more practical forms of communication. It is not necessarily impressive to use a big word where a shorter, more succinct one will do. This is also true of using foreign terms where English is preferable. When we speak or write, we should use the best words to convey our meaning.

As in all quests for change, something is lost if only the barest, most basic language is used to write a letter or carry on a telephone conversation. There are times when a writer or speaker can make a special distinction with a different word. Overuse of one word is also very boring and sometimes misleading. We want to be able to use a synonym (a word that has the same meaning); therefore, we need to know as *many* words as possible in order to fully understand and communicate in one of the richest and most forceful languages in the world—English.

Activate Your Passive Vocabulary

Changing a word from one that you vaguely know to one that you can understand and use with confidence is an important first step in strengthening your vocabulary. Here's how you can bring those passive words to life.

- Buy a notebook that is small enough to fit in your pocket or handbag.

- Always carry a small dictionary wherever you go.

- Concentrate on your *passive* vocabulary.

- Make a note of a new word and where you found it.

Ways to Turn Passive into Active

First, select at least five or six passive words each day. Read everything you can get your hands on. Pay attention to all the methods of communication: speaking, reading, writing, and listening. Each time you come across a word such as *hone*, write it in your notebook. Include a sample sentence. Now, having targeted the word, try this:

- Check the pronunciation of the word in a dictionary.
- Check the meaning of the word to be sure you are accurate.
- Write a sample sentence in your notebook, or write several sample sentences.
- Note the times you hear this word.
- Finally, begin to use the word frequently and keep a record of usage.

PRACTICE EXERCISES

What can we do to make a *passive* word *active*? The following exercises will help you to begin just such an effort.

Read the following paragraphs. Select three words that you would consider part of your passive vocabulary.

When it comes to reading a map, most of us are familiar with the United States, but how many Americans are knowledgeable about Canada? If we were asked how many provinces there are in Canada, only a few of us would give an answer with any authority.

If you said ten, you are correct. Yet, it is even more unlikely that many of us could name those provinces, which are Alberta, British Columbia, Manitoba, New Brunswick, Newfoundland, Nova Scotia, Ontario, Prince Edward Island, Quebec, and Saskatchewan (plus three territories).

After reading the previous paragraphs, go over them again and select three words that are in your passive vocabulary. The selection will differ, but let us suppose that most of you have selected the following three words:

> knowledgeable
>
> provinces
>
> authority

Look up the words in your dictionary. Check the meaning of each word if you do not already know it. Then use each one in a sentence.

1. _____

_____

_____

2. _____

_____

_____

3. _____

_____

_____

After practicing writing sentences, begin to listen for words that you only vaguely understand; you often do not even begin to hear the word until you practice using it yourself.

Be sure of your pronunciation of the new words and use them at the earliest opportunity in a conversation. Some of your friends may be surprised to hear you say something like *pundit* in an ordinary conversation, but they will be impressed when you pass that GED with flying colors.

CHAPTER 4

WORD FORMATION PRACTICES

Always try to project a positive attitude.

— Michael Jordan
former National Basketball Association (NBA) player, Olympic Gold Medalist, five-time NBA MVP

AFFIXATION

Affixation is the practice of combining prefixes (which come at the beginning of a word) such as *ab*, *de*, and *trans*, and suffixes (which come at the end of a word) such as *ful*, *able*, and *tion*, with a base word such as *port*, *astro*, or *manage*. For example, if you were to combine the word *astro* (meaning star) with the suffix *naut* (sailor), you have the word *astronaut*.

BASE WORDS

Base words are foundations for thousands of words in the English language. By adding either prefixes, suffixes, or both, you can figure out the meanings of words when you cannot find their meanings in the dictionary.

The following list contains base words in frequently used words. They will give you a reliable foundation for your work as you prepare to take your GED test. Note the meaning of these base words as they stand alone.

BASE WORDS FOR VOCABULARY BUILDING

Base	Meaning	Examples	Affixes
arch	rule	mon-*arch*-y	mon, y
cap	head	de-*cap*-i-tate	de, tate
ceive	come	re-*ceive*	re
cept	absorb	per-*cept*	per
cide	occur	co-in-*cide*	co
cord	agree	dis-*cord*	dis
creas	grow	in-*crease*	in
cred	believe	*cred*-ible	ible
dict	speak	pre-*dict*	pre
duct	guide	pro-*duct*-ion	pro, ion
fect	accomplish	ef-*fect*	ef
fer	carry	con-*fer*	con
fin	end, complete	de-*fine*	de
firm	strengthen	con-*firm*	con
fug	run	re-*fug*-ee	re, ee
grad	step by step	*grad*-u-ate	ate
ject	throw	pro-*ject*	pro
jud	judge	*jud*-i-cial	cial
lect	choose	se-*lect*	se

leg	law	*leg*-is-late	late
lit	read	*lit*-er-ate	ate
logy	study	bi-o-*logy*	bi
med	middle	inter-*med*-iate	inter
minis	serve	*minis*-ter	ter
mit	send	trans-*mit*	trans
nym	name	ant-o-*nym*	ant
ord	place in order	*ord*-er	er
pathy	state of feeling	anti-*pathy*	anti
pel	push	dis-*pel*	dis
pend	awaiting	sus-*pend*	sus
pon	put	post-*pone*	post
port	carry	ex-*port*	ex
quest	search for	*quest*-ion	ion
rect	manage	di-*rect*-or	di, or
scrib	write	*scrib*-ble	ble
script	write	*script*-ures	ures
serv	save	con-*serve*	con
spect	see	*spect*-a-cle	cle
spir	breathe	in-*spire*	in
spon	answer	corre-*spond*	corre
stat	stand	*stat*-us	us
struct	build	con-*struct*	con
sum	take up	as-*sum*-e	as
tain	keep	as-cer-*tain*	as, cer
terr	earth	*terr*-ain	ain
var	change	*var*-iety	iety
vent	come	*vent*-ure	ure
vert	turn, change	sub-*vert*	sub
vinc	win	con-*vince*	con
vis	see	*vis*-ion	ion

viv	live	re-*vive*	re
voc	call	*voc*-al	al
volv	turn	e-*volve*	e

COMPOUNDING

Another word formation practice that will increase your vocabulary very quickly is understanding *compound* words; for example, take the expression *to look for a needle in a haystack. Hay* and *stack* are actually two words, not one, but when they are combined, they make an entirely new word that means a pile or stack of hay. Another example of a compound word is putting together the two words *book* and *mark*, which gives us the compound *bookmark*.

PARTS OF SPEECH

By understanding the function of words such as nouns, verbs, adjectives, and adverbs, you can better comprehend the meanings of words and the sentences in which they appear. Here is an easy chart to help you remember parts of speech.

PARTS OF A SENTENCE

Noun: The name of people, places, things.
The sale lasted only three days.

Verb: Expresses the action of the sentence.
I read the newspaper every day.

Complement: Completes the meaning of the predicate (verb).
The teacher gave a test in class today.

Pronoun: A word that takes the place of a noun.
When she wrecked her car, Katy had to take the bus to work.

Adjective: Modifies a noun or a pronoun.

The Empire State Building is a famous building in New York City.

Adverb: Modifies a verb or another adverb.

The nurse quickly signaled code blue.

Preposition: Shows relationships between other words in the sentence.

The parade wound its way through the downtown area.

Conjunction: Connects words, phrases, and clauses.

A perfect way to learn a new language quickly is immersion and practice.

When you begin to study words by their parts, it is also important to distinguish between the various kinds of prefixes and suffixes.

GRAMMATICAL AFFIXES (INFLECTIONS)

The following table will help you to recognize the eight grammatical inflectional suffixes in the English language.

Inflectional Suffix	Example	Grammatical Function
ed	lock(ed)	past tense or past participle
en	bidden	past participle
ing	swimming	progressive form or present participle
s	plays	third person singular verb
's	doctor's	possessive
er	higher	comparative
est	safest	superlative

When we add *ed* to verbs, we have a grammatical inflection. In the case of verb tenses, we have created simple past tense; that is, *walk* is the simple present tense form of the verb, while the simple past tense of walk is *walked.* Note how the addition of the grammatical suffix *ed* resulted in making walk into simple past tense.

PREFIXES

Most prefixes also have a special function. Examples of these are the prefixes, *un, in, im, ir,* and *non.*

An easy way to conquer the spelling of these prefixes is to remember that *non* is often affixed to a word that begins with a capital letter and contains a hyphen, as in non-Turkish or non-Asian. Otherwise, these negative prefixes are found in the following combinations (and many more).

(in) dependent.
A three-year-old child is striving to be <u>independent</u>.

(im) mature.
However, three-year-olds are also very <u>immature</u>.

(ir) resistible.
Their innocence makes them <u>irresistible</u> *to their caretakers.*

Quantity Prefixes

These prefixes may be helpful in remembering mathematical terms.

Prefix	Word Derived from Prefix
(uni) one	unit
(multi) many	multiply
(bi) two	bilateral
(tri) three	triangle
(semi) half	semicircle
(poly) many	polygram

PRACTICE EXERCISE: PREFIX/SUFFIX

Underline the prefix or suffix that relates to numbers, then write a sentence using this word.

1. bicycle

   _____

2. tricycle

   _____

3. equidistant

   _____

4. tricolor

   _____

5. bilateral

   _____

Answers:

1. <u>bi</u> (two-wheeled vehicle)
2. <u>tri</u> (three-wheeled vehicle)
3. <u>equi</u> (of equal distance)
4. <u>tri</u> (three colors)
5. <u>bi</u> (two sides)

Possible Sentences:

1. William has a new bicycle.
2. Young children may learn to manage well on a small tricycle.
3. Two sides of a triangle are equidistant.
4. The French flag is tricolored.
5. An apple is bilateral.

CHAPTER 5

IMPROVING SPELLING SKILLS

Whatever muscles I have are a product of my own hard work—nothing else.

— Evelyn Ashford
Sprinter, Olympic Gold Medalist

TIPS FOR SPELLING NEW WORDS

There is no designated test for vocabulary. However, building vocabulary skills requires careful spelling in order to express one's thoughts effectively. Since most of us are not good spellers to begin with, it is even more important to learn to spell each new word as we study it. Focus your attention on spelling and you will be a good speller—or at least an improved speller—by the time you finish this book.

The second important consideration is that a number of questions on the multiple-choice section of Test 1: Language Arts Writing require the test taker to recognize correctly spelled words. Another important consideration is that spelling is a measurable element of your written essay, which is also part of Test 1: Language Arts Writing.

So, bad spelling skills can result in a very low test score in Test 1. This is of particular importance because there is a minimum score that must be achieved in each individual test, no matter what the average score of the five tests is. Still, you can improve your spelling skills. While there are no rules that cover every problem word, you can make good use of the rules that do exist. Falk S. Johnson's book, *A Self-Improvement Guide to Spelling*, is an excellent guide to spelling rules and other strategies for becoming a better speller. Other useful spelling books include Barron's *Spelling the Easy Way* and *Pocket Guide to Correct Spelling*.

Always make an organized effort to remember the spelling of all of the words you study; then you must apply every memory device you can make up. Here are a few that may help you:

- Check the word in your dictionary.
- Analyze the word.
- Picture it in print.
- Target the spelling of problem words.
- Take spelling rules seriously.
- Review, review, review!

When studying a new word, ask yourself if the word is pronounced as it is spelled; do not assume that it is. For a new word, double-check your dictionary. Remember that the diacritical (stress or accent) markings in the dictionary give you the long and short vowels, the consonants and their blends, and the main syllable stressed.

Analyzing the Word

Always examine the initial sound of the word as well as the ending sound. If the word consists of a prefix plus a base, you may be able to figure out the word without further effort. If it ends with a suffix, this will add more meaning to the word. In other words, when you are familiar with base words, you do not have to keep reinventing the wheel. The base word *cept*, for example, usually means *get* or *take*. If you add the prefix *per*, which means *through* or *by means of*, to the base, it becomes the word *percept*. When you also add a suffix, such as *ion*, which means *condition* or *act of perceiving*, you have formed the word *perception*.

Picture the New Word

Picturing a word may mean more to some spellers than to others. When you visualize the actual spelling of the word, you will learn to spell it. Should you visualize what the word means, not how it looks on a printed page, configuration may not be as helpful. An example of this is learning the word *flower*. For those who imagine a beautiful flower as they think of the word, the spelling of the word is secondary. The solution is to do both. Recall the image *and* picture the spelling of the word as well.

Target the Problem Word

Some words are simply more difficult to spell than others. You will find a number of lists for them, but perhaps the difficulty of many of these words, called terror words by some, varies from person to person. Good spellers will tell you to start your own list of words that constantly give you a problem. You may find that the word *lose* is hard for you to spell because you confuse it with the word *loose*. Make up your own list of "terror" words and study those as well as any prepared choices by other spellers.

Take Spelling Rules Seriously

Some of the most common spelling rules seem so old-fashioned that we often regard them as useless. Many of these rules, however, can cover a lot of words and provide a basis for conquering the spelling of difficult words. Although the GED tests do not evaluate a test taker's vocabulary as such, a strong vocabulary is essential for success on the test. Here are a few of the major spelling rules you might want to study (but be aware that there will always be an exception):

- Certain consonant sounds are always spelled the same way: *qu*, as in *quick*, and *wi* as in *wisdom*.
- Some consonant sounds are silent, as the *b* in *doubt*, the *k* in *mock*, and the *w* in *wrong*.
- Long vowel sounds are pronounced as if you are saying the alphabet: A - E - I - O - U.
- A single vowel that does *not* come at the end of a word is nearly always short, such as *bet*.
- If two vowels occur together, the first vowel is usually a long sound, as in *easy*.
- When combining *i* and *e* always remember that before most consonants *i* comes before *e*: *believe*, *relieve*. But *e* comes before *i* after *c*: *receive*, *deceit*.
- Drop the final *e* in a word when adding a suffix, as in *advance*, *advancing*; *advise*, *advisory*.
- But keep the final *e* in words before a suffix that also begins with a vowel, as in *knowledgeable*. Exception: *salable*.
- Substitute *y* for words that end in *ie* before adding a suffix, as in *die*, *dying*; *tie*, *tying*.
- Use the suffix *able* if the base word is a complete word by itself, as in *workable*. Exception: *valuable*.
- Use the suffix *ible* if the base word is not complete, as in *visible*, *forcible*. Exception: *collectible*.

Note: Additional spelling tips are provided throughout the list of the 400 words.

PRACTICE EXERCISES

Practice finding the ten consonants in the following words that are *not pronounced* and underline them.

1. tomb
2. listen

3. island

4. salve

5. psychology

6. sock

7. solemn

8. salve

9. wrong

10. chasten

Answers: 1. <u>b</u>   3. <u>s</u>   5. <u>p</u>   7. <u>n</u>   9. <u>w</u>
             2. <u>t</u>   4. <u>l</u>   6. <u>c</u>   8. <u>l</u>   10. <u>t</u>

Add the suffix *able* to the following words:

1. profit   _____

2. work   _____

3. manage   _____

4. employ   _____

5. do   _____

Answers: 1. profitable   4. employable
               2. workable   5. doable
               3. manageable

Give the plural form for the following words:

1. opportunity   _____

2. city   _____

3. delay   _____

4. county   _____

5. baby   _____

Answers: 1. opportunities   4. counties
             2. cities   5. babies
             3. delays

The rule *i* before *e* except after *c* usually guides us in correct spelling. Look at the following five words and place an X following any word that is correctly spelled.

1. percieve   _____

2. believe   _____

3. science   _____

4. receive   _____

5. breif   _____

Answers: 1 and 5 are incorrectly spelled.

CHAPTER 6

WORDS THAT GOOD READERS NEVER MISS

Age is whatever you think it is. You are as old as you think you are.

— Muhammed Ali
former U.S. heavyweight boxing champion

MODAL AUXILIARIES

Though often called modals for short, *modal auxiliaries* are helping verbs that are used with other verbs to complete their meanings. Modal auxiliaries are especially important in building vocabulary skills because they are small words that are essential in communicating certain modes or conditions of expression.

Consider the words *can, could, may, might, should, had better, must, will,* and *would.* These are frequently used modals. They do not always appear in a vocabulary skills book, yet their meanings are varied and they are important to the understanding of more complex sentences.

Modal	Meaning	Sample Sentence
can	ability	Betty's friend can fly a single-engine airplane.
can't	inability	Betty can't stand to fly in small planes.
can	possibility	Perhaps I can go to the movies with you tonight.
could	possibility	This summer could be very hot.
couldn't		It couldn't be hotter than last year.
may	permission	May I help you cook dinner?
may not		No, you may not.
may	possibility	David may go to law school next year.
may not		His wedding may not take place.
might	possibility	He might get there early.
might not		The mechanic might not have time today.
will	certainty	The new apartment will be big enough for us.
won't		This vacation won't be too expensive.
will	willingness	The principal will give the invocation.
won't		She promises that she won't take more than five minutes to do the work.
will	request	Will you come to my house tonight?

won't		Sally promises she won't charge more than five dollars an hour to babysit.
must	necessity	The journalist must meet his deadlines.
have to	necessity	The children have to be careful while playing outside.
have got to	necessity	I have got to catch the last bus home.
must	logical deduction	The alarm clock is ringing, so it must be time to get up.
should	necessity	I should take my umbrella today because it is going to rain.
would	conditional	He would do it if he had the money.

PRACTICE EXERCISES: RELATIONSHIPS
Exercise 1

Study the following sentences. In the column on the left, place the word you believe is the modal auxiliary in the first blank. In the second blank, give the meaning of the modal.

Example:

(Modal)   (Meaning)

<u>could</u>   <u>possibility</u>

I could never sing in public.

(Modal)   (Meaning)

1. _____ _____

Each student in the class must give a report on a magazine article.

2. _____ _____

The class will then question the speaker and can make comments.

3. _____ _____

Some students thought they could try to discredit the speaker by their questions.

4. _____ _____

He won't get a very good grade because he did not practice his speech before giving it in front of the class.

5. _____ _____

John knows he might have to do some extra work because he was absent when his classmates gave their reports.

6. _____ _____

The class in life skills is required but many students do not know why they cannot take another subject instead.

7. _____ _____

The principal explained that students must take certain courses because they are required by the state board of education.

8. _____ _____

Communication skills must be important because most schools have them in their curriculum.

Answers:
1. must, necessity
2. can, ability
3. could, possibility
4. won't, certainty
5. might have to, possibility
6. cannot, inability
7. must, necessity
8. must, necessity

Exercise 2

Supply the missing word with an appropriate modal auxiliary.

1. That _____ mean a thing. (won't, should)

2. The mayor _____ approve but we're not sure. (may not, couldn't)

3. You _____ need to hurry. (won't, should)

4. Steve _____ work very hard in order to attend community college. (must, can't)

5. The authorities feel that the cause of both fires _____ be the same. (could, should)

6. The boys _____ be dependable by now. (should, can)

7. The poor results of his efforts _____ be disappointing to his family. (must, should)

8. This is a boring article and _____ not have been written. (can, should)

Answers:
1. won't
2. may not
3. won't
4. must
5. could
6. should
7. must
8. should

PART TWO

ESSENTIAL WORDS
FOR THE GED

HOW TO USE THE WORD LIST

More than 400 essential words on the following list form the second part of this book. Many of them were selected from the GED Practice Tests. Others were chosen from TV news broadcasts, periodicals, and newspapers, and from a sampling of high school textbooks and other literature.

Each listing is arranged alphabetically and indicates whether it is a noun, pronoun, adjective, adverb, or verb. The meaning of the word is followed by a sample sentence. The dictionary used for the word list was *Merriam-Webster's Collegiate Dictionary, Tenth Edition.*

You may want to select ten or fifteen words each day. As you study, take the time to write the word, spell it, think it, say it, and make the word yours. Spelling and grammar tips are also included to give you additional support as you study.

WORD LIST

A

aberrant *adj.* not according to normal standards.

(science) *The cell was easily recognized by its* aberrant *movements.*

(political) *Suspected terrorists are more easily identified if they belong to a known* aberrant *group.*

abdicate *v.* to voluntarily give up a high office or other important responsibilities.

Britain's King Edward VIII announced that he would abdicate *his throne to marry the woman he loved.*

absolute *adj.* (science) undiluted, or having full strength, without any watering down.

Absolute *zero is a theoretical temperature that is characterized by the absence of heat.*

(general) relating to a degree of strength or an unconditional status.

The chairman wanted absolute *power over his committee without any interference from others.*

Spelling Tip: New Words

Repeating the word aloud will help you to remember the word at a later time. It will also help you to learn to spell the word so that you can add it to your vocabulary for future writing and speaking.

---

absorb *v.* (science) to take in and make part of an existing whole.
Water is absorbed *by a plant's root system.*

(social) to give complete attention to something.
Some TV shows can so absorb *young children that they don't hear anything else.*

abstract *v.* to select, or take from.
He decided to abstract *his report from a much longer paper.*

abstract *adj.* something that is more theoretical than real.
Jeff would rather read an adventure novel than abstract *poetry.*

abutment *n.* solid wall constructed to counteract a lateral thrust; also the place where a joining occurs.
The abutment *to the bridge had deteriorated over time and could no longer act as a barrier.*

acceptable *adj.* adequate, capable, but not outstanding.
On a scale from one to ten, I give that movie a five because it is barely acceptable.

accord *v.* to award, to grant, or to bring into agreement.
The Purple Heart is one of the oldest medals accorded *individuals wounded in military action.*

accord *n.* an agreement, such as that reached in a treaty or a binding understanding.
Many South American countries have reached accords *with Fidel Castro while the United States continues to boycott Cuba.*

Usage:
Always know what part of speech you wish to use when looking up a word in the dictionary. The meanings of a word will differ according to the part of speech.

---

accurate *adj.* (social) free from error; conforming to the truth.

Small business owners usually hire an accountant to prepare an accurate *financial statement for banks and for the Internal Revenue Service.*

(science) exact and correct; conforming to a standard.

The results of the DNA tests have become extremely accurate.

acid *n.* a substance in a solution with a pH less than 7; derived by partial exchange of replaceable hydrogen.

Boric acid *can be used as an antiseptic.*

acidic *adj.* (science) acid-forming.

The process of making steel involves the use of furnaces lined with acidic *materials.*

(social) used metaphorically to mean sharp, sour in manner.

The store owner's wife drove away customers with her acidic *manner.*

acumen *n.* a sense of sharp perception or shrewdness, especially in practical matters.

Women in the workplace are proving that they possess as much business acumen *as their male counterparts.*

adapt *v.* (literature and arts) to draw upon an original piece to create a completely new one.

The film Huckleberry Finn *was* adapted *from author Mark Twain's book of the same name.*

(social) to make fit for new use by modification.

It is not always easy to adapt *to a new culture.*

addition *n.* increase; to combine numbers in order to achieve a simple quantity.

The addition *of baking powder to a mixture of flour and water causes the dough to rise.*

adjacent *adj.* (general) in the close vicinity of or actually touching.

The price of the house for sale included an adjacent *garage.*

(geography) referring to common borders.

Canada and the United States have the longest adjacent *border without military presence in the world.*

adjective *n.* a word used in grammar; describes a noun or a pronoun.

In the sentence, "The lawyer bought a new computer for her office," the word "new" is an adjective.

ad-lib *v.* spoken without preparation or restraint.

Actors sometimes ad-lib *their lines in a performance to cover a mistake.*

admonish *v.* to scold gently.

The teacher admonished *her fifth-grade class for not handing in their homework on time.*

adverb *n.* a word that tells how, when, where, or how much, and modifies verbs, adjectives, other adverbs, prepositions, clauses, and phrases.

Many adverbs *end in ly, such as quickly, happily, sadly.*

aggravate *v.* to intensify a situation that is already unpleasant or negative; to arouse displeasure.

When the landlord raised the rent for the third time that year, he aggravated *the tenants' already hostile feelings.*

Spelling Tip:

Note the difference in the spelling of aggravate and aggregate; one is *gra* and the other is *gre*.

---

aggregate *n.* the sum or parts of something that are loosely related.

Sometimes an aggregate *of declining numbers results in experts in the stock market predicting a bear market.*

aggression *n.* a forceful action or an intentional action to dominate or master.

When Hitler's troops seized Austria in 1938, Germany was accused of unnecessary aggression.

allegory *n.* a work of literature or art in which the components, figuratively or symbolically, represent human characteristics.

Many of Aesop's Fables *are considered* allegories *because they contain characters that represent good and evil.*

alloy *n.* mixture of base metals; a mixture that results in lessening the value of the original.

Gold jewelry is an alloy *of two metals; the more unmixed gold it contains, the more valuable it is.*

alter *v.* to change from one thing to another without modifying something else.

The criminal dyed his hair black and had plastic surgery to alter *his original good looks.*

alternative *n.* a choice.

College athletes realize that one alternative *to engaging in professional sports is teaching athletics at a school.*

ambivalent *adj.* having a simultaneous and contradictory feeling or attitude toward a person, place, thing, or action.

The people can be ambivalent *toward political leaders; sometimes they admire them and sometimes they reject them.*

amnesty *n.* a pardon granted to a large group of people.

Amnesty is sometimes granted in order to release prisoners of conscience as long as they have not violated other individuals or committed physical abuse.

analogy *n.* similarity of some aspects of two or more things.

One might draw an analogy *between the movements of the hands of a clock and the sun sweeping across the sky.*

analyze *v.* to study various parts and determine their relationships.

(chemical) *Chemists are trying to* analyze *the effects of rain containing high proportions of acidic properties.*

(social) *It is important to* analyze *every aspect of a problem before coming to a decision.*

anachronism *n.* anything that is out of place in time.

A television antenna on the roof of a house in a Civil War movie would definitely be an anachronism.

anarchy *n.* absence or denial of any government; state of lawlessness.

Following the American Revolution, military leaders feared complete anarchy.

ancient *adj.* relating to something that happened hundreds or thousands of years ago; relating to a time early in history; describing an artifact or piece of art that is very old.

Everyone knows that the use of fireworks dates back centuries to ancient *China.*

annex *v.* to add to, expand, or supplement.

Japan annexed *Korea several years before World War II.*

anonymous *adj.* not named or identified.

Many generous contributors to a cause often prefer to remain anonymous *by not having their names made public.*

anterior *adj.* located near the front or the head.

One method of preparing an insect collection is to push a pin through the anterior *portion of the insect.*

anthology *n.* a collection of stories, art, music, or other written creative pieces.

I just bought the new anthology *of Shakespeare's sonnets.*

anthropomorphism *n.* the condition of an animal having human characteristics.

An example of anthropomorphism *is the Cheshire Cat in* Through the Looking Glass.

apartheid *n.* political and economic segregation against non-Europeans in South Africa.

Apartheid *was responsible for thousands of deaths in the 1960s and 1970s in South Africa.*

apocalypse *n.* a revelation, especially a prophesy, of the end of the world.

Many feared the Cold War would heat up and lead to an apocalypse *and total destruction of our civilization.*

appease *v.* to agree to something in order to avoid conflict.

Before World War II, Britain was accused of attempting to appease *Adolf Hitler in order to avoid war.*

appropriate *adj.* suitable; fitting a special use.

Using slang in a formal speech is not considered appropriate.

approximate *adj.* (mathematics) nearly correct or exact.

The problem called for an approximate, *not an exact, solution.*

arc *n.* something arched or curved; something that forms an electrical arc or follows an arch-shaped course.

The arc *of the enemy's missile was visible across the sky.*

archetype *n.* the original or most typical.

Tom Wolfe's book The Electric Kool-aid Acid Test *is considered an* archetype *of the hip generation, as it portrays the young people of the time and their culture.*

arouse *v.* to awaken from sleep; to stimulate.

The lion was aroused *by the hunter's footsteps and began to roar.*

asexual *adj.* relating to reproduction by cell division, spore formation, fission, or budding, not involving a union of individuals or cells.

The amoeba is asexual; *it consists of one cell that divides into a new cell, thus creating another amoeba.*

associate *v.* to keep company with; to combine, join, or relate.

The councilman advised his wife to associate *only with people who could help him win the election.*

astute *adj.* to show shrewdness.

Because of their astute *pronouncements, many judges are regarded as wiser than they are.*

attribute *n.* a praiseworthy characteristic.

It is customary to include your most positive attributes *in a job application.*

attrition *n.* an indirect reduction in numbers resulting from death, resignation, or transfer.

The botany class was so difficult that it had a higher rate of attrition *than the class in environmental studies.*

authoritarian *adj.* relative to a system of complete control by a central head.

Feudal systems relied upon obedience to an authoritarian *form of leadership.*

autobiography *n.* a work of nonfiction that is based on the writer's own life.

Famous people often hire a ghostwriter to help them with their autobiographies.

auxiliary *adj.* functioning in a subsidiary capacity.

The Parent Teacher Association (PTA) is a strong auxiliary *group in both private and public schools.*

axiom *n.* expression or self-evident truth; an established rule or principle.

Many health care providers continue to tell their clients that the saying "an apple a day keeps the doctor away" is an axiom *they can trust.*

axis *n.* a straight line about which a body or a geometric figure revolves.

Students are sometimes asked to determine the axis *in a particular geometry problem.*

B

ballad *n.* a simple and sometimes sentimental song that tells a story.

Many ballads from the American Civil War tell of individual heroism.

bar graph *n.* something that is drawn to transmit information in a visual pattern of vertical symbols.

The bar graph *published by the computer store illustrated several good reasons for owning a personal computer.*

barrier *n.* something material that blocks or intends to block free movement, or that separates certain substances; it may be real or metaphoric.

Many students are discouraged when they encounter certain barriers *to attending the college of their choice.*

base *v.* to form; to serve as a support.

The book A Tree Grows in Brooklyn *was* based *on the author's childhood in a New York City borough.*

base *n.* a fundamental part of something or a main ingredient.

The manufacturer discovered a less expensive base *for its paint that was just as reliable as the original.*

basic *adj.* fundamental; relating to or forming the base or essence of something.

In the early 1950s, women often wore basic *black with pearls.*

behavior *n.* a manner of conducting oneself.

The fans' unruly behavior *at the baseball game disturbed the visiting team's performance.*

being *n.* a living thing or a state of existence.

The frightened children took their parents to see the strange being *in the swamp.*

benefit *v.* promoting the well-being of something.

Dr. Schweitzer's work in Africa benefited its people and earned him their gratitude.

benign *adj.* describing a situation or individual that is kind and gentle; harmless.

Fortunately, the results of the patient's laboratory tests showed the tumor to be benign and no surgery was necessary.

bias *n.* a prejudgment or prejudice of a situation, person, or idea.

The university's decision to cancel many of its bilingual courses is believed to reflect a bias against foreign nationals.

bile *n.* a secretion of the liver that is stored in the gallbladder.

Bile is essential to the digestive process, aiding in the absorption of fats.

bill *n.* (business) list of items or services charged to the consumer.

I was dismayed by the number of calls listed on my phone bill.

   (political) a plan for a law that's written and voted upon.

The State House of Representatives is debating a bill that will raise personal property taxes.

binary *adj.* (math) a system of counting in computers where only 0 and 1 are used.

I cannot interpret the binary coding on the printout.

   (science) consisting of two elements or parts.

It is called binary fission when the cell divides into two equal parts.

biography *n.* a book about a particular person's life.

Some readers prefer biographies to fiction because they are more interested in a narrative based upon a real individual.

blasphemy *n.* irreverence toward something considered sacred.

Blasphemy *was considered a crime and was severely punished in early years of Christianity.*

body *n.* the main part of a plant or an animal; the main part of a piece of writing or manuscript.

Although the letter had a hostile tone to it, the body *of the missive alleviated the reader's anxiety.*

bondage *n.* a state of being bound by compulsion; tenure of service in early colonial days; the state of a slave.

The difference between the bondage *of an indentured servant and that of a slave was that the servant had a certain time allotted to his* bondage, *while a slave was never free from birth until death.*

boondoggle *v.* to create a worthless or senseless job in order to provide benefits to workers.

Politicians have been accused of boondoggling *in order to win an election, only to cancel the worthless jobs later.*

boundary *n.* a line, a point, or a plane that indicates or fixes a limit.

Many disputes in new African nations have resulted from disagreements over boundaries.

boycott *v.* to refuse to have dealings with someone or to express disapproval.

In the 1950s, some condominiums were known to boycott *new renters because they did not want the apartments open to people of other races.*

brainstorm *n.* a bright idea; a process by which writers create ideas for stories or essays.

The students formed groups of three or four in order to discuss ideas and come up with a brainstorm *for their reports.*

burgeoning *adv.* not yet fully grown; future promise.

The burgeoning *legislation was meeting serious resistance in the House of Representatives.*

budget *v.* to anticipate future needs for money or time.

Sometimes it is hard for parents to budget *their money following the arrival of a new baby and all the expenses that entails.*

butt *n.* often used as another word for target.

The new office worker was upset at being the butt *of many of his coworkers' jokes.*

C

calculate *v.* to measure something using numbers; to determine quantities or to solve specific problems using numbers.

By calculating *an acceptable payment schedule, the bank determined that our loan and interest will be paid off in two years.*

candidate *n.* someone who runs for office or who applies for a position with a company.

Alexander seemed a likely candidate *for the job before the employer discovered he was under twenty-one.*

capitalism *n.* an economic and social system where most businesses are owned and operated by individual citizens, not by the government.

The business community in the United States was built on capitalism.

capitulate *v.* to yield; to give up after negotiations.

The sudden arrival of armed troops forced the opposition to capitulate.

carnivore *n.* an animal that eats meat.

Are giraffes carnivores *or do they eat only plants?*

cast *n.* the list of actors and actresses in a movie, TV, or theatrical production.

The entire cast *and the production crew were treated to a party by the theater management.*

century *n.* a period of 100 years.

The Norman soldiers invaded what is now England in the eleventh century.

character *n.* a person in a novel, play, poem, or other literary art form.

The character *of Captain Bligh in the book* Mutiny on the Bounty *has become symbolic of the tyranny of commercial ships' officers in the late eighteenth century.*

circumference *n.* the distance around a circle or an object that is round.

The circumference *of the earth is approximately 25,000 miles.*

civil *adj.* relating to a nonmilitary activity or set of laws in business, education, and other activities; polite.

Diane's brother was married in a civil *ceremony.*

civil disobedience *n.* action by a group of people who are protesting government actions, usually in a nonviolent manner.

India's Mahatma Ghandi believed in nonviolence and developed methods of civil disobedience *that have served as models for other countries.*

clause *n.* a group of words that contains a subject and a verb and is part of a sentence; a section of a formal document.

In a sentence, two independent clauses *must be connected with a conjunction such as* but *or* and.

Grammar Tip:

Clauses that can stand alone are *independent clauses;* those that cannot stand alone are referred to as *dependent.*

---

climate *n.* a characteristic pattern of weather that includes temperature, rainfall, snowfall, wind, and other prevailing conditions.

Countries bordering the equator are more likely to have warm climates *and year-round growing cycles.*

climax *n.* a major turning point; the highest point of a play or other art forms.

During World War II, British troops were rescued from the beaches of Dunkirk, providing a welcome climax *to a near disaster and loss of the British Expeditionary forces.*

> **Grammar Tip:**
> It is incorrect to join two or more sentences with only a comma; this is called a *comma splice.* Example: It is raining, I must remember my umbrella. Correction: It is raining. I must remember my umbrella.

communism *n.* a system of government in which goods are owned in common, thereby eliminating private property.

Communism was once the official doctrine in the former Soviet Union but more and more people have now opened their own businesses.

compare *v.* to judge or to examine two or more ideas or things to show how they are different or how they are similar.

Michael found it difficult to write a paper that compares *the Vietnam War with the Persian Gulf War.*

compatible *adj.* existing together without causing problems; able to operate computer programs on different computers.

It was important that the software provided by the company be compatible *with the PCs that other firms were using.*

component *n.* a part of something.

The laboratory staff worked several weeks to identify the missing component *of the formula.*

compound *n.* something that is composed of two or more parts.

It was difficult for the laboratories to determine the chemical compounds *of the drugs found by the police until they studied all of their parts.*

concept *n.* an idea or an understanding arrived at with higher thinking skills; an abstract idea.

The concept *that the earth was round took many years for the general public to accept.*

conciliatory *adj.* to become friendly or agreeable.

The council was conciliatory *when it appealed to the towns-people for an increase in taxes.*

conclusion *n.* the last part of something; that portion of a composition that summarizes or reiterates the thesis of the writing.

The essay was very clever and had a particularly exciting conclusion.

concrete *adj.* referring to an argument or idea that is based on facts.

The political candidate rarely speaks in any concrete *terms, but instead depends on rhetoric and hyperbole.*

confront *v.* to meet face to face; to oppose.

If the politician confronts *the issue instead of sidestepping it, she will win the election.*

connection *n.* the relationship between ideas, people, or cultures.

During her first years in public school, Maria found that her Hispanic culture provided an important connection *with other students from the same background.*

connotation *n.* the indirect or inferred meaning of a word or a group of words.

The act of perjury can be a connotation *of guilt.*

consensus *n.* general agreement.

A consensus *of opinion among the medical staff resulted in an early cure for the disease.*

conservation *n.* careful and practical use of our world's resources.

Environmentalists are urging global conservation *before it is too late for the earth.*

construct *v.* to build; to join together ideas, words, phrases, or sentences to convey certain meanings.

The legal team constructed *a new defense for their client.*

contemporary *adj.* associated with modern times; of the present.

Many of the themes of the classics continue to have a contemporary *appeal.*

contraction *n.* combining two words into one.

It is better to avoid contractions *such as* isn't *and* don't *in more formal writing.*

contrast *v.* to compare articles, people, places, or things to show how they are different.

If we contrast *early rock-and-roll performers with more recent artists, we can appreciate how far this form of music has developed.*

Grammar Tip:

When contracting a word, an apostrophe is substituted for one or more letters. One can say *isn't* (the contraction for *is* and *not*) in conversation but it is not advisable in a written examination.

---

cube *n.* a solid object containing six equal sides; the number arrived at when a number is multiplied by itself twice.

The cube *of 4 is 64.*

culminate *v.* to reach a climactic or decisive point.

Industrial barons of the early twentieth century built railroads throughout the country as a culmination *of westward migration.*

current *adj.* presently happening or being used.

The crime rate for the current *year is significantly lower than last year's rate.*

current *n.* (geography) directional flow of water in lakes, rivers, or oceans.

Ocean currents *may be caused by the passage of air over the water.*

(science) the flow of an electrical charge.

The current *in a lightning strike is dangerous to people in its area of intensity.*

(aeronautical) the part of a fluid body (as air) moving continuously in a certain direction.

The air currents *were so rough that the pilot asked passengers to fasten their seat belts.*

cyberspace *n.* the many connections between computers in different locations, such as a place where messages, pictures, information exist.

Whenever we consider the capabilities of the Internet, we think in terms of cyberspace.

cyclical *adj.* moving in cycles.

A woman's life often appears to move in a more cyclical *manner than that of a man.*

cylinder *n.* a chamber in a pump from which the piston expels the fluid.

The mechanic at the garage traced the problem with the car to the cylinder *because the gasoline could not be ignited there in order to drive the piston.*

cynic *n.* one who believes that conditions are at their worst and that people are only interested in their own well-being.

Michael is becoming such a cynic *about the economy that his friends avoid talking about money with him.*

D

data *n.* measurements, statistics, and other factual information used as a basis for reasoning, discussion, or calculation.

An earlier collection of data *was helpful when the task force started the new project.*

dearth *n.* an inadequate supply of something.

There is a dearth *of building space in Manhattan.*

decade *n.* a period of ten years.

The 1930s was a decade *of economic deprivation.*

decadent *adj.* declining or crumbling into disuse; referring to widespread self-indulgence.

The Roaring Twenties was considered a decadent *era when many individuals acted without inhibitions.*

decrease *v.* to lessen, reduce.

The landlord has decreased *the store's rent by 10 percent because of road construction near the building.*

deduce *v.* to determine by deduction; to infer.

The family deduced *from his bruises that their child was being bullied at school.*

defend *v.* to save from danger; to take action in the face of an attack.

John Paul Jones was an eighteenth-century naval officer who defended *the colonies' important ports.*

definitive *adj.* providing a final solution or definition; authoritative; describing a perfect example.

The expert's paper on the stock market proved to be the definitive *thesis.*

deity *n.* supreme being; a god.

Eugene O'Neill's play The Emperor Jones *portrays a man who has persuaded others to accept him as a* deity, *not as an ordinary man.*

demagogue *n.* a leader who acts on existing prejudices.

Hitler was a clever demagogue *playing upon the biases of his constituency.*

democracy *n.* a form of government in which vital decisions are voted on by all eligible citizens and the majority rules.

The United States operates as a democracy, *a system in which power is vested in the people through their elected representatives.*

demographics *n.* information about human population that is relevant to science or to commerce, or referring to the identification of markets.

Unless the demographics *are favorable, new products are not released for sale.*

denotation *n.* direct and specific meaning of something.

The results of the clinical study were explicit and provided a direct denotation *of the committee's work.*

derivative *n.* something drawn from or flowing from a common source.

Belladonna is a drug derivative *of foxglove, a common garden flower.*

derive *v.* to draw from a common source.

Some of the colonists' ideas of freedom were derived *from the writings of Thomas Paine and other patriots.*

desiccate *v.* to become dried up.

When a plum desiccates, *it becomes a prune.*

despot *n.* a ruler with complete control and power.

Napoleon Bonaparte, a French despot *of the late eighteenth century, was exiled to the island of St. Helena where he died in 1821.*

deteriorate *v.* to degenerate and become inferior.

Confidence in the U.S. military deteriorated *following the Japanese attack on Pearl Harbor and had to be rebuilt.*

develop *v.* to slowly elaborate and make clear; to execute step-by-step.

The new business program at the community college was developed *over a period of two years.*

device *n.* a method by which the writer or artist achieves predicted results.

Novelist Toni Morrison is well known for using carefully structured scenes as a device *to build characterization.*

diagram *n.* a drawing that shows relationships and summaries, and contains pictorial information.

A diagram, *like a picture, can be worth a thousand words.*

dialogue *n.* a conversation between two or more people; the conversational components of a literary and dramatic composition.

Neil Simon, the renowned playwright, was admired for the witty dialogue *in his plays.*

Punctuation Tip:

Written dialogue is enclosed in quotation marks usually with a comma or period inside the closing quotation mark; for example, "I think you have my gloves," said Janet when she saw it was snowing.

---

dictator *n.* a leader holding absolute power.

Although Native Americans once relied on their chief for final decisions, this leader was in no way a dictator; *everyone had a say.*

diction *n.* vocal expression; enunciation.

The diction *of TV newscasters is a significant part of their effectiveness.*

dictum *n.* a formal pronouncement of a principle or decision.

The dictums *issued by Julius Caesar in the early history of the Roman Empire are still quoted and studied in this century.*

didactic *adj.* relating to the act of teaching.

Educators often wish to avoid appearing overly didactic *and try to be more interesting in their approach.*

dimensions *n.* measurements; outlines.

The stage dimensions *were much smaller than the cast was used to.*

diorama *n.* a carefully sculpted scene that sometimes includes small figures and other realistic details.

The diorama *the class made of the Pilgrims' first Thanksgiving was donated to the public library.*

discreet *adj.* careful, prudent, not hasty.

One expects one's physician to be thorough and to be most discreet *in diagnosis and treatment.*

discrete *adj.* (not to be confused with *discreet*) unconnected, separate, and distinct.

The school system is still guided by the dictum that religion and education are to be separate and discrete.

disenfranchise *v.* to deprive of a constitutional or statutory right, usually in elections.

Until 1920 and the ratification of the Nineteenth Amendment, women in the United States were disenfranchised *and unable to vote in local or national elections.*

disseminate *v.* to spread around; to disperse.

Many early socialists were intent on disseminating *their message throughout the country.*

dissolution *n.* the act of separating something into component parts; liquefying or breaking down.

Rapid dissolution *is usually necessary in developing medicine that is taken by mouth.*

distinguish *v.* to separate into kinds, classes, or categories.

Some essay questions could require the writers to distinguish *between informal and formal communication.*

distribute *v.* to hand out; to divide according to predetermined guidelines.

NATO discourages distributing *or selling weapons to countries hostile to their neighbors.*

divide *v.* separating into two or more parts; determining how many times a number contains another number.

The easiest numbers to divide *are even numbers.*

divisible *adj.* capable of being divided.

Even numbers are divisible *by the number 2.*

dogmatic *adj.* arrogantly overbearing.

The professor was not well liked because of his dogmatic *lectures.*

domestic *adj.* referring to goods or products that are produced by one's own country.

While the United States leads many countries in its domestic *exports, it lags behind in trade agreements with some foreign powers.*

dominant *adj.* referring to a genetic character or factor that is stronger than others.

It is a proven fact that certain genes are more dominant *than others.*

dominate *v.* to have a commanding position or to completely rule or control.

The theory that one twin tends to dominate *the other is just that—a theory.*

dormant *adj.* in a state of suspension; temporarily devoid of action.

Sometimes viruses lurk in one's system in a dormant *condition and do not appear for years.*

duplicity *n.* deceptive words or actions.

Such duplicity *soon earned the attorney a bad reputation.*

durable *adj.* able to exist for long periods of time without deteriorating.

Denim was invented in Nîmes, France, and grew to be a favorite material for work clothes because it is so durable.

duration *n.* a measurement or length of time.

The President of the United States, once elected, is referred to as Mr. President for the duration *of his life.*

E

easement *n.* land owned by another that entitles its holder to limited use.

The easement from the town square to the lake was badly in need of repair.

eccentric *adj.* deviating from an established style or expectation of behavior.

Many businesses have a dress code and are less tolerant than others of eccentric *dress.*

eclectic *adj.* referring to a combination of styles that creates fresh approaches to certain projects, particularly in the arts; sometimes used to indicate a combination of certain qualities.

Certain mid-nineteenth-century architectural styles were considered eclectic *because they combined past historical styles.*

ecology *n.* the study of relationships of various organisms and their environments.

Ecology focuses on the interactions of certain animal and plant life with their physical surroundings.

ecosystem *n.* the physical environment of plants, animals, and microbes.

Several types of sponges grow out from the underside of coral, which supplies an ecosystem *that is supportive to their development.*

edify *v.* to instruct spiritually.

His purpose was to edify *the family to improve its image within the neighborhood.*

egocentric *adj.* limited in outlook and needs; relating to one's own needs with a disregard for others.

The student was so egocentric *that he thought of no one but himself and his perception of the class was therefore distorted.*

egregious *adj.* obviously bad or inflammatory.

The action was deemed egregious *and quickly covered up by the department.*

electorate *n.* a body of people entitled to vote.

The electorate *in some societies is requested to vote only in the official language.*

electronic *adj.* relating to electrons.

Most musical groups today include electronic *instruments, such as guitars, basses, or pianos.*

element *n.* one of the four substances: air, water, fire, and earth; any fundamental substance consisting of atoms.

Chemical elements *contain a specific number of atoms, such as carbon, whose atomic number is six.*

elicit *v.* to draw forth.

The purpose of posting the magazine's advertisement subscription rates was to elicit *a response from its readers.*

eliminate *v.* to get rid of; to expel.

To stay afloat, the passengers on the lifeboat were forced to eliminate *extra cargo.*

ellipse *n.* a closed plane curve generated by a point moving in such a way that the sums of its distances from two fixed points is a constant; also can refer to an oval.

The rear of the White House faces Pennsylvania Avenue, but the front of the President's residence looks out over an ellipse.

eminent *adj.* standing out; of high regard or office; designating a powerful office.

The mayor insisted that his closest advisors defer to him and continue to regard him as the most eminent *member of the group.*

emission *n.* the discharge of substances into the air.

Strong laws have been passed in most states regarding emissions *from automobiles and trucks that pollute the air.*

empower *v.* to delegate official authority or legal power to; to enable.

The pastor's sermon empowered *the church members to pass new rules of conduct for the congregation.*

emulate *v.* to model oneself after; to excel or to try to equal in achievements.

The circus was filled with exceptional feats of all kinds that children tried to emulate *once the performers left town.*

energy *n.* (general) a vigorous exertion of power or effort.

The energy *of the young children soon exhausted the adults taking care of them.*

(science) usable power such as heat or electricity.

The universe is dependent on solar energy.

engender *v.* to cause to happen; to create.

The quarterback on the high school football team engendered *the admiration of his classmates.*

epigram *n.* a short, witty saying.

One of the many epigrams *of President Abraham Lincoln that continues to be popular is, "My father taught me to work; he did not teach me to love it."*

epilogue *n.* a concluding section; a final but short scene of a play that summarizes the main action.

Many narrative poems end with an epilogue.

epitome *n.* an embodiment of or a brief form.

The beautiful china set was the epitome *of the family's effort to maintain its status among friends and family.*

equator *n.* a great circle around the earth that is equidistant from the two poles.

The equator *divides the earth into the northern and southern hemispheres.*

equitable *adj.* fair; fair-minded; exhibiting a sense of equality.

Recent changes in hiring practices have resulted in much more equitable *conditions for women and people of color seeking jobs.*

equity *n.* the difference between assets (money that is debt-free) and liabilities (money that is owed).

When buying a home, some owners double payments some months, so the equity *will build more rapidly.*

erosion *n.* slow deterioration of a substance or product.

When trees are cut down in large numbers, the soil that remains is likely to be diminished by erosion.

essay *n.* a literary composition with a point of view that is developed into a thesis.

Although Stephen King is famous for his occult novels, he has also written many nonfiction articles and essays.

Usage Tip:

A writer who confines his writing to essays is known as an *essayist*. Essay writing is often more interpretive than didactic and can also be used to indicate a trial or attempt at creating something.

---

essay question *n.* an examination question that requires an answer either in a sentence or a paragraph.

The midterm examination consisted of four essay questions *as well as multiple-choice questions.*

existential *adj.* closely associated with existence; (literary) referring to a twentieth-century movement in the arts that encouraged individual responsibility not based upon rules of right or wrong.

Although the existential *school of art appeared to reject much of the past, it also depended on the artist's past experience.*

exonerate *v.* to judge someone free of guilt; to restore a person's reputation to its former status.

In the lawsuit the lawyer asked the court not only to award money in return for his client's pain, but also to exonerate *the plaintiff of any wrongdoing.*

exorbitant *adj.* excessive; more than justified; outside appropriate limits.

The resort's exorbitant *prices soon gave it a reputation for being a playground of the rich and famous.*

exposition *n.* a discourse or statement that reveals or discusses meaning, facts, information, and explanations.

The homework assignment was to write an exposition *detailing the school's policies regarding absenteeism.*

expository *adj.* referring to a classification of names, classes, and types of writing; referring to a style of writing, particularly when discussing nonfiction presentations.

Many students do not regard expository *writing as challenging as fiction writing.*

extrovert *n.* one who is unreserved and receives gratification outside oneself.

It may be hard for a person who is an extrovert *to form a relationship with someone who is very quiet.*

F

facetious *adj.* not serious; inappropriately funny.

The teacher was being facetious *when she told her students that she would send them to the principal's office if they did not quiet down.*

facile *adj.* superficial; easy; insincere.

The editor told the reporter that his writing was facile *and accused him of not doing adequate research.*

faction *n.* a group of people, often hostile.

The opposing faction *was causing a lot of trouble in the department.*

farce *n.* a satirical, light drama that is marked by broad humor and silly situations; sometimes used on stage to suggest that a real-life situation is like a farce.

The employees thought the strike was a farce *and did not take it seriously.*

fauna *n.* animal life characteristic of a region.

New building developments in rural areas are threatening the region's fauna *and flora.*

fervor *n.* with passion; intense feeling.

The fervor *of the attack on the English soldiers came as a great surprise after General Washington's audacious crossing of the Delaware River.*

figurative *adj.* expressing something through a symbol or a metaphor.

She said she was going out of her mind with worry, but we knew that was just a figurative *statement.*

filibuster *n.* the use of tactics to promote delays or action in a legislative group to prevent a decision.

Many of the senators resented the use of a filibuster *by the members of the opposing party to delay a vote on the proposed legislation.*

finesse *v.* to skillfully handle a situation.

When office space was reassigned, the director's assistant was able to finesse *a corner suite with three windows.*

fine-tune *v.* to adjust carefully in order to achieve the best level of performance.

The surgical team would not operate on patients until they had fine-tuned *their techniques.*

fissure *n.* a narrow opening or crack.

Following an earthquake the survivors must be very careful to avoid newly formed fissures.

flagrant *adv.* especially severe and hostile.

Before the raid was over, Union soldiers covered dozens of miles through flagrant *Confederate encampments.*

focus *n.* a point of concentration.

The PTA meeting's focus *was on eliminating drug use in the schools.*

foreshadow *v.* to suggest what will happen later.

Most novelists foreshadow *what will occur in a mystery novel by adding warnings in the beginning of the book.*

fossil *n.* evidence of an organism from the distant past.

Great excitement resulted from the discovery of an ancient fossil *during a field trip.*

fraction *n.* a small portion.

There was only a fraction *of the original investment remaining after years of neglect.*

fractious *adj.* unruly or troublesome.

The visitor was so loud and fractious *that her host vowed never to invite her again.*

fraternal *adj.* relating to or involving brothers.

A fraternal *organization such as the Elks emphasizes the close relationship of its members.*

frugal *adj.* thrifty, often to a fault.

Edith was so frugal *with her money that she often missed out on having a good time.*

fulminate *v.* to issue a denunciation; to attack.

The family members fulminated *against every attempt by the inept accountant to make good on the loss they had suffered.*

futile *adj.* having little or no hope.

It was obvious that a team effort was futile *at this point because they were so far behind in the game.*

G

garner *v.* to accumulate; to save; to collect.

The awards garnered *by the more sports-minded fraternity members rested on the fireplace mantle in their house.*

garrulous *adj.* talkative; wordy.

If a filibuster is needed in the U.S. Senate, the most garrulous *senators are called upon to speak.*

genre *n.* a kind or sort; a category of artistic, musical, or literary composition.

She was most familiar with the mystery genre *of television drama.*

genteel *adj.* having an aristocratic quality; having a special style.

The nineteenth-century aristocrat strived to be elegant, free from vulgarity, and genteel.

germane *adj.* relative and appropriate.

The book club will not discuss literature that is not germane *to its objectives.*

gerund *n.* a part of speech used in a sentence as a noun; a present participle.

You get a gerund *by adding* ing *to a stem word, as in* swimming.

glut *n.* an inordinate or excessive amount.

When wheat crops are good, wheat becomes a glut *on the market.*

grandiose *adj.* exaggerated in a ridiculous manner.

The new school board had grandiose *plans for public schools under its direction.*

gratify *v.* to indulge or satisfy; to reward.

Owning certain products will gratify *the pride of some shoppers.*

gratuitous *adj.* giving or rendering services without charge.

When a doctor performs surgery without charging a fee, it is a gratuitous *service.*

graven image *n.* an object of worship usually carved from stone or wood.

Some religions forbid worshiping any graven image *other than that of their own deity.*

gravity *n.* (general) solemnity, seriousness.

When the fire alarm rang, the visitors lingered in the hall because they did not realize the gravity *of the situation.*

(science) the attraction of the mass of the earth, the moon, or other planets for smaller bodies at or near their surfaces.

During its flight into space, the orbiter Discovery *no longer is subject to the earth's* gravity.

guile *n.* cunning; full of tricks; unreliable.

The advertising agency has sometimes been accused of being misleading by using guile *in their advertising copy.*

H

hackneyed *adj.* overused, trite.

The school yearbook was resplendent with hackneyed *words of praise.*

hamper *v.* to impede, close, or prevent from happening.

The Allied invasion of Europe in 1944 was hampered *by stormy weather.*

harass *v.* to constantly annoy or threaten someone.

When the new city manager began to receive calls meant to harass *her, she called the police.*

harbinger *n.* something or someone that foreshadows what is to come; a precursor.

American folklore regards the groundhog as a harbinger *of spring.*

harness *v.* to control and use the natural forces and power of something.

When Hoover Dam was built in the 1930s, it harnessed *enough power to irrigate much of the state of Nevada and make it an area of industry and tourism.*

hearsay *n.* rumor; evidence presented in court that reports someone else's experience.

The evidence given by the witness was considered hearsay *and therefore had to be stricken from the court records.*

hedonism *n.* the doctrine that pleasure is the most important element of one's life; complete absorption in finding happiness to the exclusion of all else.

Many people believe that artists who embrace hedonism *are not serious about life, without realizing the sacrifice they must make to achieve excellence in their field.*

helix *n.* something spiral in form; a coil formed by winding a wire around a bulb.

The detection of the construction of the double helix *found in nucleic acids led to the discovery of DNA.*

herbivore *n.* an animal that eats only plants.

The giraffe is a herbivore *whose long neck enables it to eat from the tops of taller plants.*

heresy *n.* adherence to a religious opinion contrary to church dogma.

Many of the settlers who made their way to the New World in the seventeenth century had been accused of religious heresy *in their home countries.*

hiatus *n.* a break or interruption in time or tenure.

After a considerable hiatus *because of ill health, the mayor returned to his duties.*

hibernate *v.* to pass long periods of time in a torpid state.

While it hibernates, *the North American brown bear's body temperature drops significantly.*

hierarchy *n.* a classification of people according to ability, status, and authority; a ruling body or clergy; a division of angels.

The game of chess is based on certain religious and military hierarchies *with pieces named for kings, queens, knights, and bishops.*

The office of conference chairman is the fourth-ranking position in the hierarchy *of leadership.*

high-energy *adj.* yielding a lot of energy.

Peanuts are recognized as a high-energy *food source.*

highlight *v.* to direct a strong light toward something; to center attention; to become an important aspect or the most interesting of something.

The Degas exhibition was highlighted *by his self-portrait, the most important part of the show.*

homogenous *adj.* made entirely of one substance.

The children appeared homogenous *in their gym clothes.*

hypothesis *n.* unproved theory.

Scientific research is usually preceded by a hypothesis *that is later proven.*

hypothetical *adj.* relating to conjecture or supposition; containing a hypothesis.

Let's say that this situation is hypothetical *and has not been proven.*

I

ideology *n.* ideas about human life and culture.

The political candidate's anti-war ideology *during the war in Vietnam lost him a number of important votes.*

idiosyncrasy *n.* an odd behavior pattern; a set of peculiar characteristics.

Among the librarian's idiosyncrasies *was the habit of speaking in a whisper to all of the library's patrons.*

idol *n.* a symbol of worship; an object of devotion.

Many religious rituals include the worship of certain idols.

idolize *v.* to show extreme partiality for; to adore.

The child idolized *his grandfather and looked up to him as a role model.*

illicit *adj.* not legal, forbidden.

During the Great Depression of 1929, sale of illicit *alcoholic beverages was severely punished by the U.S. government.*

impartial *adj.* not partial or biased.

The jurors found it difficult to remain impartial *throughout the embezzlement trial.*

imperial *adj.* relating to an empire or to royalty.

Princess Diana did not like to appear imperial *and was called the "people's princess."*

imperialism *n.* a policy of extending influence over a country with the intention of taking control of its economic and political matters.

Great Britain's imperialism *was at its peak when it ruled many smaller countries.*

implement *v.* to follow through or to see that something is done.

The city council found it easy to pass the zoning regulations but found it difficult to implement *them.*

impotent *adj.* powerless; helpless; unable to perform.

The relief crew felt impotent *when it realized it could do nothing about the destruction caused by the earthquake.*

improvise *v.* to make, invent, or arrange without previous preparations.

The hikers had to improvise *when they were stranded without supplies in the mountains.*

impugn *v.* to attack or denigrate the integrity of a person, a leader, or a country.

Britain's Prime Minister Neville Chamberlain refused to impugn *the Nazi leader, Adolph Hitler, regarding his brutal attack on Austria.*

inadequate *adj.* not enough, insufficient.

During World War II, there was an inadequate *supply of penicillin for civilian patients.*

inappropriate *adj.* not proper; not at all helpful; misguided.

The teacher's practice of writing with a marker on the forehead of a forgetful student was deemed an inappropriate *punishment by the principal.*

inaugurate *v.* to be formally inducted into office; to begin.

In 1865 George M. Pullman inaugurated *the use of railroad cars with comfortable furnishings for day travel and convertible sleeping berths for night trips.*

incite *v.* to instigate or urge to action.

Before the Revolutionary War, colonists were accused of inciting *riots and encouraging their fellow citizens to demonstrate against the Crown.*

incongruous *adj.* inconsistent; not conforming; lacking propriety.

Encouraging parents to report their children to the police on trivial matters is incongruous *with upholding family values and instilling trust.*

incredible *adj.* hard to believe; improbable.

The incidences of multiple births since the development of fertility treatments is incredible.

increment *n.* expansion; one in a series of units.

The increment *of ten digits may go back to early humans counting on their fingers and toes.*

inert *adj.* very slow to move or act; scientifically, lacking in active properties.

The gas was inert *until exposed to heat.*

infamous *adj.* having a bad reputation; causing or convicted of a crime bringing infamy.

Lizzie Borden is said to have committed one of the most infamous *crimes of the nineteenth century—the brutal murder of her father and stepmother.*

infer *v.* to guess; to surmise.

It is often possible to infer *a solution to a problem, but not without carefully looking at the facts*

infinitive *n.* the base verb preceded by the word *to*; examples: to run; to make.

Grammar Tip:
When possible, avoid splitting infinitives. <u>Wrong</u>: Try to always follow up a reservation with a confirming phone call. <u>Right</u>: Always try to follow up a reservation with a confirming phone call.

inherent *adj.* intrinsic to or an essential part.

An inherent *characteristic of children is curiosity.*

intervene *v.* to interfere; to come between.

It appeared that the children would be separated when their parents died until their grandmother intervened *and took them both home with her.*

introduction *n.* the part of a writing that presents the thesis of the composition.

A strong introduction *can prepare the reader for the rest of the composition.*

introverted *adj.* describing one who is self-sufficient and who looks inwardly for satisfactions.

An only child might end up introverted *because of lack of satisfactory relationships with other people.*

irony *n.* a way of expressing something that implies a contradiction of what is actually being said; a style of writing.

The dramatic irony *of the play showed the playwright's sardonic view of mankind.*

issue *n.* a specific controversy.

His decision to leave the university before completing his degree became a serious issue *with his family.*

J

jeopardy *n.* the act of being placed in a dangerous position or situation.

General George Washington placed his dwindling troops in jeopardy *when he crossed the Delaware River in bad weather to attack the British on Christmas Eve.*

judge *n.* one who sits in judgment.

After weighing the evidence presented to the grand jury, the judge *decided to try the young girl as an adult.*

judiciary *n.* the system of courts of law and/or their judges.

Although the young boy could have been tried as a minor, the decision of the judiciary *was to charge him as an adult.*

jugular *n.* the most vital or vulnerable part of something.

The contestants did not hesitate to go for the jugular *when it came to scoring against their competition.*

juggernaut *n.* an unrelenting campaign or force that crushes whatever is in its path.

The Crusades were a juggernaut *of Christian soldiers who invaded the Holy Land during the eleventh, twelfth, and part of the thirteenth centuries.*

junta *n.* a group of people who seize control of a government.

There was widespread rioting after the junta *came into power in the South American country.*

juxtapose *v.* to place side by side.

It is not accurate to juxtapose *the American colonies' Revolutionary War with the U.S. Civil War.*

K

kangaroo court *n.* a mock court where the guidelines of justice and law are disregarded.

The proceedings were more like those of a kangaroo court than those of a legitimate court of law.

keynote *adj.* the central or most dominant.

The president usually delivers the keynote address for the conference.

kinetics *n.* the mechanism by which a physical or chemical change is effected.

Kinetics is a branch of science in which the minute particles of substance are in vigorous motion.

kismet *n.* fate.

The simplest way to avoid taking responsibility for one's actions is to be fatalistic and ascribe them to kismet.

knowledgeable *adj.* exhibiting intelligence.

The person hired to answer the phones was friendly as well as knowledgeable.

L

labyrinth *n.* a place full of twists and turns and blind alleys; something intricate and perplexing.

The actor offered a labyrinth *of excuses and denials for not knowing his lines.*

lance *v.* to pierce; to open with a sharp instrument.

The country doctor performed simple surgery, such as lancing *infected areas, on the kitchen table.*

latent *adj.* not fully developed.

The eighth grade chorus consisted of many latent *talents.*

latitude *n.* freedom of action or choice.

Choosing a place to be married has become one of wide latitude*, with some couples selecting boats, planes, and even motorcycles.*

legacy *n.* something transmitted by an ancestor or predecessor.

The will contained several legacies *of property, jewels, and money for the lucky beneficiaries.*

lethal *adj.* relating to or capable of causing death.

It was a lethal *accident that could have been prevented.*

lethargic *adj.* lazy; indifferent; in a physical or mental stupor.

The extremely high temperatures of southern countries can often be held responsible for the lethargic *behavior of the inhabitants.*

liberate *v.* to free; to allow be at liberty.

During World War II, the Allies liberated *civilians who had been held prisoner.*

liege *n.* a vassal; a person bound in feudal service.

There are societies in the world that still renounce independence and adhere to the feudal system of liege *and lord.*

M

machination *n.* a scheming, devious plan with some evil result.

The widow did not discover her boyfriend's machinations *until he stole all her money.*

malinger *v.* to fake an illness to avoid work.

Malingering *to avoid military service is punishable by a prison sentence.*

malleable *adj.* shaped with little effort.

Gold is a malleable *metal.*

mandate *n.* a formal order or authorization.

Several states have issued mandates *to preserve the mangrove trees that help form barriers against hurricanes.*

manifest *v.* to show or make easily understood or recognized.

Until the rains manifest *themselves, the weather in September in the central Great Plains of the United States is unusually dry with only occasional scattered thunderstorms.*

Usage Tip: manifest

Manifest is a word with two very different meanings; check the part of speech you intend to use.

---

manifest *n.* a list of passengers or list of cargo for a vehicle or plane.

Suspicions still exist about the actual cargo versus that listed on the manifest *of the Lusitania, a British ship sunk off Irish shores during World War I.*

manipulate *v.* (science) to operate with the hands or mechanically in a skillful manner.

Orthopedists must expertly manipulate *the affected area of the body.*

(general) to control by artful and deceitful means to one's own advantage.

When Eva Peron and her husband assumed control of Argentina, they manipulated *their constituency at every opportunity.*

manuscript *n.* a written or typed document as opposed to a printed one.

The scientist plans to submit the manuscript *of his book to the publisher at the end of the week.*

marginal *n.* bare minimum; small measure of difference.

The cost of the property was marginal.

maritime *adj.* relating to the sea.

At the beginning of the Civil War, the Confederates had no maritime *power to employ against the North's naval blockade.*

martyr *n.* a person who willingly chooses death as a penalty; one who makes a sacrifice for the sake of principle.

Joan of Arc was a martyr *who chose to die because of her religious beliefs.*

maxim *n.* a well-known phrase or saying that teaches us a lesson.

The maxim, *"Early to bed and early to rise makes a person healthy, wealthy, and wise," may still be valuable advice today.*

member *n.* a part of a group; a part of the body of a plant or animal.

Some species have the ability to regenerate a lost member *such as a claw or an eye.*

mentor *n.* an experienced person who helps another who is less knowledgeable.

The community college matched new students with mentors *to help them during the first few weeks of classes.*

metaphor *n.* a word or phrase denoting something similar.

"Today the sea is a boiling cauldron" is an example of a weak and overused metaphor.

microcosm *n.* a world or community that is regarded as a small part of another world; the same world but in a greatly diminished size.

Some people believe that Atlanta, Georgia, has grown to become a microcosm *of New York City.*

misanthropic *adj.* describing anyone who hates mankind; mistrusting; cynical.

Charles Dickens' story about Christmas portrays the character of Scrooge as a misanthropic *tightwad.*

mitigate *v.* to lessen; to make less severe or painful.

Half-measures will not help or mitigate *the terrible devastation of the tropical storm.*

modify *v.* to make minor changes.

The Wright brothers modified *their bicycles to achieve more speed.*

modulate *v.* to adjust or to keep in proper proportion.

The singer had to modulate *her voice when the accompanist changed the key.*

mollify *v.* to soothe or to ease.

In ancient times the crow was a symbol of discord and strife, and, up to the present time, people's fear of this bird has still not been mollified.

monarchy *n.* a system set forth in a constitution in which a king and queen are the ceremonial heads of state but the decision-making process is carried out by elected officials.

During the last century many monarchies *reduced their royal members' duties and power.*

monologue *n.* a dramatic speech in poetic form; a theatrical presentation performed by a single actor.

Will Rogers was a beloved entertainer who was famous for his monologues *about life in the United States.*

musician *n.* one who performs music as a soloist or as a member of a small group or a large orchestra or band.

The musicians *were on stage with their instruments during the blackout.*

N

nebulous *adj.* of cloudlike quality; not precise; not concrete.

After considering many nebulous *production methods that were not described in writing, the company decided not to proceed.*

nepotism *n.* favoritism in making governmental or business appointments.

Nepotism *often involves sons, daughters, nieces, nephews, and other relatives who receive special favors or jobs.*

nihilism *n.* the view that all past traditions and practices are useless and stupid; the complete rejection of past values.

In renouncing the traditions of their forebears, many artists embraced nihilism *during the twentieth century.*

nocturnal *adj.* happening at night; describing animals that are active at night and sleep during the day.

The raccoon, a nocturnal *carnivore that forages at night and sleeps all day, has adapted to urban life.*

nominal *adj.* existing in name only; insignificant.

The honorarium offered to the speaker for her keynote address was so small as to be considered nominal.

nostalgia *n.* a sentimental recollection of the past; some types of literature that are based not on factual recall but on a more satisfying and sometimes humorous improvement of the past.

The author Booth Tarkington was known for including nostalgia *in his essays and short novels about his boyhood.*

notorious *adj.* describing one who has achieved fame, but unfavorably.

Many sports figures have earned notorious *reputations for their behavior off the field or court, and are no longer admired by the fans.*

novel *n.* an invented narrative of human experience through a sequence of events and scenes and carefully executed characters.

When President Lincoln met Harriet Beecher Stowe, and referred to her novel, *Uncle Tom's Cabin, he commented, "So this is the little woman who started a war!"*

noxious *adj.* physically harmful; deadly; morally corruptive.

When the fire spread to the other rooms of the house, the noxious *fumes awoke the sleeping family.*

nuance *n.* subtle varieties of colors, voicing, writing, and other art forms.

Although she was still a student, there were many nuances *in her cello solos that were seldom achieved by older performers.*

nutrient *n.* something that nourishes and promotes growth.

The lack of nutrients *in the food supply can stunt children's growth during a drought.*

O

oblique *adj.* obscure; devious.

His oblique *remarks were insulting and not based on the facts.*

obscure *v.* to be made indistinct, not easy to understand.

A good mystery has a strong plot that should not be obscured *by too many deviations and false clues.*

olfactory *adj.* relating to the sense of smell; in literature, referring to writing that appeals to the sense of smell.

Even though the advertising copy for the perfume was not great literature, it had examples of olfactory *imagery.*

oligarchy *n.* a system in which a country is governed by individuals not elected by its citizens.

Ancient Rome was ruled by an oligarchy.

ombudsman *n.* one who investigates reports or complaints and suggests possible solutions.

Many businesses have an ombudsman *as well as a customer service department to deal with customer complaints.*

ominous *adj.* foreboding; possible evil.

The warnings were more ominous *than first believed.*

omnipotent *adj.* all powerful; having unlimited knowledge or authority.

The Incas were convinced that their gods were omnipotent *beings and controlled everything.*

omnivore *n.* (science) one that consumes both animal and plant life.

Human beings are classified as omnivores *because they feed upon both animal and plant substances.*

(metaphorical) enjoying everything.

Lincoln was an omnivorous *reader who often read far into the night.*

options *n.* alternatives; choices made available.

The prospective client was pleased with the many options *offered in the new policy.*

orthodox *adj.* conforming to an established belief or dogma; relating to any conservative religious belief.

Their relationship was forbidden by their orthodox *beliefs.*

outline *n.* a shape or outer boundary of something; also a condensed form of information, usually involving numbers and letters to designate different points.

The outline *had to be approved before the paper was written.*

P

pacify *v.* to placate; to calm.

The only way to pacify *the child was to sing a favorite song.*

panacea *n.* a remedy for all ills or problems.

The discovery of antibiotics was welcomed as a panacea *for humankind.*

pandora's box *n.* the mythical box sent by the gods that released mankind's evils upon the world.

By delving into the bank's affairs, the investigator was said to have opened a pandora's box.

paradigm *n.* something that is typical; an excellent example.

The paradigm *had been carefully prepared by the scientists for presentation to their colleagues.*

paradox *n.* something unexpectedly puzzling; a contradictory statement or communication.

Airline regulations for carry-on luggage have become such a paradox *that many passengers call in advance for an explanation.*

parody *v.* to ridicule; to make fun of.

When the students parodied *the school superintendent in their class play, they were disciplined for their insolence.*

paternal *adj.* of or pertaining to fatherhood.

More and more courts are responding to paternal *claims in which the father wants more rights regarding his child.*

pathology *n.* the study of the nature of diseases.

Thanks to advances in pathology *since 1900, we can expect to drink reasonably safe water in our cities.*

patronize *v.* to treat cooly; to be condescending toward.

My aunt has found that the men at her garage patronize *her because they think that, as a woman, she doesn't understand anything about cars.*

pedantic *adj.* boring; overly scholarly.

The instructor managed to avoid a pedantic *explanation to the new formula.*

pejorative *adj.* referring to unflattering or demeaning attitudes or remarks.

She was insulted by her employer's constant pejorative *remarks about her weight.*

penchant *n.* a special preference and continued use of something.

It was soon apparent that the inebriated young minister had a penchant *for the elderberry wine made by his parishioners.*

peremptory *adj.* final, dictatorial.

The peremptory *announcement soon halted the resistance forces.*

perennial *adj.* present at all seasons of the year; enduring, persistent.

Due to a perennial *interest, the chamber orchestra planned one concert each year to include Beethoven's "Moonlight Sonata."*

perjure *v.* to swear under oath to what is untrue.

The officer was close to perjuring *himself before his attorney advised him to tell the truth.*

perturb *v.* to throw into disorder or mayhem; to upset.

The children's antics did not seem to perturb *their calm parents.*

peruse *v.* to read or examine something in a thorough way.

Jane loves to go to a bookstore and carefully peruse *the books on the best-seller list.*

pervade *v.* to penetrate and overrun at an astonishing rate.

During the 1950s, the United States became alarmed when Communism appeared to pervade *the country.*

phonetics *n.* a system of speech sounds.

Hooked on Phonics *is based on the practice of teaching reading mainly through* phonetics *rather than word configurations.*

photosynthesis *n.* the formation of carbohydrates in the chlorophyll-containing tissues of plants exposed to light.

The theory of photosynthesis, *in which plants take in carbon dioxide and give off oxygen, was developed in 1898.*

Spelling Tip:
Words or syllables that contain the *f* sound are often spelled with *ph,* such as *phrase* or *phonetics.*

---

phrase *n.* a meaningful arrangement of words with or without a subject and a predicate.

The letter consisted of phrases, *not complete sentences.*

phrase *v.* to write something in a certain style or with a special purpose.

He did not know how to properly phrase *his question when he decided to ask his girlfriend to marry him.*

piety *n.* the quality of being pious.

When certain religious groups established colonies in North America, settlers were often judged not only by their wealth but by their piety.

pious *adj.* showing devotion; marked by intense reverence.

During the Middle Ages, European churches demanded a pious *response from their parishioners.*

pivotal *adj.* having the ability to turn as if on a pivot; crucial.

A rich supply of potassium, which is pivotal *to growth, can be found in ashes from wood fires.*

placate *v.* to appease; pacify.

NATO refuses to placate *terrorists when negotiating for the release of hostages.*

plagiarize *v.* to steal someone's ideas or words without acknowledging their source.

Do not plagiarize *another's work by omitting proper citations.*

plebeian *n.* one of the common people (sometimes used as a demeaning term).

The snobbish newcomer criticized her neighbors when she referred to them as plebeians.

polarize *v.* to break up into opposing factions or groups.

Some divisive issues can cause the country to polarize.

portent *n.* something that foreshadows an amazing or ominous event.

One of the reported portents *for the birth of Jesus Christ was the brilliant star of Bethlehem.*

pragmatic *adj.* relating to practical affairs rather than intellectual or artistic matters.

The new president's idealistic views were refuted by the college's professors for not being pragmatic *enough.*

precedent *n.* a previous example; something having prior significance.

The school set a precedent *when they admitted both men and women to the faculty.*

prevail *v.* to triumph; to overcome and to become more effective.

The custom prevails *in present-day Wampanoag families of southeastern Massachusetts for a baby to sleep on a flat board laced with rawhide.*

primordial *adj.* persisting from the beginning; fundamental.

When visiting a primordial *rain forest, it is as though one is going back to prehistoric times.*

prioritize *v.* to list or arrange in order of importance.

Sometimes it becomes difficult for the newly inducted soldier to prioritize *the demands of his sergeant.*

pristine *adj.* unspoiled and uncorrupted by civilization; unpolluted; in perfect condition.

The family's Koran was in such pristine *condition that it looked like it had never been used.*

prohibitive *adj.* tending to restrain or stop.

People in the neighborhood refused to shop at the new store because the prices were so high they were prohibitive.

prolific *adj.* very fruitful; producing large numbers of works of art such as books or paintings.

With her large body of work, Pearl Buck is considered one of the world's most prolific *novelists.*

prologue *n.* a short opening scene preceding the first act of a play; action that comes before the major event.

The Spanish Civil War was a prologue *to World War II.*

promiscuous *adj.* casual to the point of being irresponsible, especially in sexual activities.

Her wild and promiscuous *behavior earned her a bad reputation.*

promulgate *v.* to make an open declaration; to decree.

President James Monroe promulgated *the Monroe Doctrine in 1823.*

proselytize *v.* to teach; to convert someone to one's beliefs.

My aunt believed that a person's religion was a private matter and refused to join other church members who wanted to proselytize *their religion by preaching at the shopping mall.*

prostrate *adj.* lying face down; overcome or overwrought.

After waiting for the parade to begin, several children were prostrate *from the extreme July heat.*

protagonist *n.* a leading character with whom the audience sympathizes; one who champions a cause.

George Smiley is the protagonist *in several of John Le Carre's spy novels.*

proximity *n.* closeness; nearness.

The city's poor live in close proximity *to the newly gentrified city slums.*

punctuate *v.* to use special marks to make the meaning of sentences and phrases clear.

When the teacher wrote directions on the board, she always punctuated *her instructions with several exclamation points!*

Punctuation Tip:

Periods (.), question marks (?), and exclamation points (!) are used at the ends of sentences to distinguish between a simple statement, a query, and an emphatic remark. Commas are used for a variety of reasons, including pauses in thought and relationships among ideas.

---

pundit *n.* a learned writer or speaker who gives opinions; one who is authoritative.

During the Civil War, pundits *from both the North and South predicted an early end to the war.*

Q

Spelling Tip:
The following words are pronounced as a blend of *k* and *w*, or *kw*, but are spelled with the letters *qu*.

quadrangle *n.* a flat shape that has four straight sides.

The dormitories were grouped around a beautiful park in the form of a quadrangle.

quadrant *n.* a quarter of a circle.

Washington, D.C., is divided into four quadrants: *northeast, southeast, northwest, southwest.*

quagmire *n.* an area of soft wet mud; a situation filled with difficulties.

It was such a poorly written mystery novel that the reader sometimes felt lost in a quagmire *of vague clues and meaningless red herrings.*

qualitative *adj.* relating to value as opposed to amount.

The professor indicated that she wanted qualitative *not quantitative reports on the use of sanctions in the Middle East.*

quandary *n.* dilemma; state of being puzzled and unable to decide.

The bride and groom were in a quandary *about how many guests to invite to their wedding.*

quash *v.* to smash; to nullify.

The parents tried to quash *the rumors that their son had stolen apples from the neighbor's tree.*

querulous *adj.* whining; full of annoying questions.

If the children missed their naps, their parents were sure they would be querulous *and cranky for the rest of the day.*

query *v.* to submit a formal question; to ask for a suggested course of action.

The student queried *the teacher about the forthcoming exam.*

quintet *n.* a group of five musicians performing together.

John was pleased to join his four friends and make up a string quintet *to perform at the holiday concert.*

quixotic *adj.* idealistic; impractical.

It is quixotic *of my friend to believe that all people want peace.*

R

rapport *n.* a genuinely friendly, trusting, and easy relationship.

Happily, the rapport *between the little girl and her new foster family was immediate.*

rapprochement *n.* the increasing of or the resumption of friendly relations.

Some pundits pinpoint the beginning of the rapprochement *of China and the rest of the world with the international Ping-Pong games held there.*

rebuke *v.* to scold; to criticize for wrongdoings.

The new CEO rebuked *his staff for tardiness.*

rebut *v.* to refute; to show strong reasons that something may be false or inappropriate.

The officer tried to rebut *his superiors' orders to execute one of his men believed to be innocent.*

recalcitrant *adj.* resistant; lacking the desire to obey or cooperate.

The stubborn and recalcitrant *lions refused to go back into their cages.*

reciprocal *adj.* mutual; exchangeable; describing a formal agreement based upon equal benefits for each group.

Russia made a reciprocal *trade agreement with China during the early 1960s that helped both countries.*

redundant *adj.* repetitious; describing someone or something that is declared unnecessary.

The strike took place after one hundred workers were told they were redundant *and would be dismissed.*

> **Usage Tip:**
> Using too many words to describe or to create an effect when a few words would do just as well is termed *redundant* and should be avoided.

refute *v.* to expose a falsehood.
Despite the council's efforts, they could not refute *the allegations.*

reiterate *v.* to repeat, often in written form and in different words.
It is always possible to reiterate *your main ideas in the conclusion in order to emphasize a point.*

reprehensible *adj.* deserving censure or extreme disapproval.
The cruel manner in which some pet stores take care of animals is reprehensible.

reprisal *n.* the act of resorting to force, short of war, to punish another nation or to retaliate for an action.
The victims of the bombing demanded reprisals *for the attack on the hospital.*

repudiate *v.* to deny or recant; to reject as untrue or unjust.
The company's president repudiated *the union's charges as soon as they were made public.*

requisite *adj.* essential or necessary.
A passport will be issued after the requisite *paperwork is submitted.*

resolute *adj.* determined; strong-willed; unrelenting.
The police were resolute *in their promise to find the bank robbers.*

rustic *adj.* rural; unsophisticated.
Many of his contemporaries considered Mark Twain rustic, *but he was far more sophisticated than they realized.*

S

sacrilege *n.* a terrible act against a hallowed place or person or thing.

When the priest found that someone had defaced the church walls, he was appalled at the sacrilege.

sanguine *adj.* optimistic; hopeful.

The physician encouraged his patients to be sanguine.

sarcasm *n.* bitter, angry speech that twists a simple phrase to mean the opposite of its meaning.

Peter's sharp tongue and constant sarcasm *placed him and his job in jeopardy.*

sardonic *adj.* mocking; derisive.

Some of the artist's paintings reflect his own cynicism by showing subjects with a sardonic *smile.*

scrupulous *adj.* having moral integrity; thorough; strictly observing right from wrong.

The hospital was scrupulous *in keeping track of the newborn babies so that no tragic mistakes could be made in the nursery.*

scrutinize *v.* to examine carefully; to take great care to observe and evaluate.

We must be sure to scrutinize *applications of the newly hired employees for misleading or inaccurate information.*

sedition *n.* insurrection against lawful authority.

Several of the rebels were finally caught and jailed for sedition.

seduce *v.* to lead astray by false promises.

The elderly are sometimes seduced *by fast-talking salesmen into investing their savings in bogus or false property.*

seize *v.* to take over; to confiscate.

Jean heard that many older homes were about to be seized *by the city council because of back taxes.*

silhouette *n.* a solid outline without detail.

As an art form, silhouettes *are sometimes used in modern art, photography, and movies.*

simile *n.* a comparison of two like things; a figure of speech; sometimes considered a metaphor that contains the word "like."

The simile *"like World War III had broken out" to describe a large commotion is overused.*

slander *n.* spoken (oral) false charges that defame and muddy one's reputation.

She sued her neighbors for slander *after they spread damaging information about her.*

solar *adj.* deriving from or relating to the sun; measured by the earth's course in relation to the sun.

There is a lot of interest among conservationists in developing solar *sources of energy.*

solvent *adj.* able to pay one's debts.

He was finally solvent *and out of debt.*

sonnet *n.* a poem consisting of 14 lines.

John Milton wrote the sonnet *that ends, "They also serve who only stand and wait."*

soporific *adj.* immensely boring.

The papers were so soporific, *they did not generate action.*

spawn *v.* to produce many eggs; to bring about the existence of something.

Salmon swim hundreds of miles in order to reach a special place where they spawn.

species *n.* a group of animals or plants of the same kind that can be bred and produce young together; a biological subdivision.

Certain species *of animals and plants are heartier and stronger than others.*

squalor *n.* filth, oppressive living conditions.

The committee hoped to clean up the squalor *of the older sections of their city.*

square *n.* a rectangle with four equal sides; one who is conventional or conservative.

He was such a square *that he was considered unsophisticated by his peers.*

stigma *n.* a mark of failure or other unattractive attribute.

Being unable to read is a stigma *as well as a handicap that is hard to overcome.*

stigmatize *v.* to disgrace or speak of another group or individual in detrimental terms.

The family stigmatized *their neighbors by making them the brunt of their jokes.*

strife *n.* violent conflict; difficulties in one's life.

The newly formed government continued to experience strife *in its dealings with the opposition party.*

structure *n.* something having form or a plan.

The structure *of her work was unmistakable in its orderliness.*

stymie *v.* to stand in someone's way; to interrupt or obstruct.

The doctor was stymied *by the many regulations of the physicians' group with which he was associated.*

subject *v.* to cause to endure.

Prisoners of war were subjected *to cruel treatment at the hands of the enemy.*

Usage Note: subject
Pay particular attention to this word; the meaning changes with the pronunciation.

---

subject *n.* a word or group of words that denotes what a sentence is about.

When you have identified the subject *of a sentence, you should then determine the predicate or verb.*

subjugate *v.* to conquer; to control.

The purpose of the new regulations was to subjugate *the union workers to the will of the owners.*

substantive *adj.* considerable; important; opposite of trivial.

When two families are merged, substantive *changes affect all family members.*

subtle *adj.* not easily perceived; delicate; refined.

Although the editorial message was subtle, *the newspaper editors thought it carried an important message.*

subvert *v.* to overthrow; to undermine.

Several suffragettes were accused of subverting *the war effort during their 1918 fight to obtain the right to vote.*

suffix *n.* a grammatical term placed at the end of a word to give it more meaning or even a different meaning.

A common suffix is -able, indicating that something can be successfully accomplished.

suffrage *n.* the right to vote.

Susan B. Anthony (1820–1906), who supported women's right to vote, fought for suffrage for more than sixty years.

superficial *adj.* shallow; relating to a thin surface; poorly developed.

The candidate's dissertation was so sketchy that it was regarded as superficial and was refused by his committee.

superfluous *adj.* unnecessary, excessive.

After all the discussion on the point, any further explanation on the principal's part was superfluous.

support *v.* to back up beliefs with facts, illustrations, or examples; to advocate.

When writers plan compositions, they try to support their theories with enough facts to make the writing credible.

surreptitious *adj.* acting or doing something secretly, with questionable motives; clandestine.

The surreptitious transfer of the patient from a designated hospital to an inferior nursing home has been challenged by her family.

sycophant *n.* a person who uses false flattery to advance himself or herself.

Several department heads tried to take over the meetings, but these sycophants were soon recognized for their efforts.

syllogism *n.* an argument consisting of a major and a minor premise followed by a conclusion; in general terms, a crafty or manipulative communication.

Advertising writing sometimes is filled with syllogisms that need to be tested before they are accepted.

syllable *n.* a single consonant sound.

It will help your spelling if you divide words into syllables.

synthesis *n.* bringing together several parts to form a whole.

Combining the best of the artist's creation was a lucky synthesis of his genius.

T

tangential *adj.* touching lightly; peripheral.

Her past experience was only tangential *to the job she was applying for, but it was close enough to impress the interviewer.*

tangible *adj.* having to do with the sense of touch; able to be appraised and evaluated; perceptible.

The lawyers hoped their client's apology gave the court a tangible *sense of his sincere regret for his crime.*

tantalize *v.* to tease; to arouse desire.

Norman Bel Geddes designed a tantalizing *view of the "World of Tomorrow" for New York's 1939 World's Fair.*

tantamount *adj.* equivalent in value or significance.

Winnning the prize money from the raffle was tantamount *to receiving a week's pay for the employees.*

temperate *adj.* moderate; restrained; mild, associated with moderate climate characteristics.

Once the travelers arrived in West Africa, they suffered from the heat because they were no longer in a temperate *zone.*

tempt *v.* to entice to do wrong; to provoke or to create an uncontrollable desire.

Although Daphne was on a strict diet, she was tempted *by the lavish dessert tray.*

Usage Note: tempt

Do not overlook derivations of this word, such as temptress (one who tempts) and temptation (the state of being tempted).

---

tenacious *adj.* cohesive, tough.

Sally is such a tenacious *shopper that she exhausts anyone who accompanies her to the mall.*

tentative *adj.* not fully formulated; hesitant; uncertain.

Because Margaret had made tentative *plans for the weekend, her daughter postponed a surprise birthday party.*

terse *adj.* short; brief.

President Lincoln's Gettysburg Address was terse *compared to the other speeches of the day.*

thesis *n.* the main idea of a written composition.

The board members considered the thesis *of his new book too radical to continue his work with them.*

topic *n.* the general area or interest of a piece of writing or a special presentation.

The topic *of the annual meeting was global education strategies.*

traipse *v.* to trudge wearily.

After spending all day walking on the golf course, Ellen's brother did not feel like traipsing *through the museum with her.*

transform *v.* to change in composition or structure.

When anesthesia was perfected, it transformed *surgical techniques, allowing for longer periods of time for a doctor to operate on a patient.*

transient *adj.* fleeting; passing quickly into and out of existence, fame, or particular notice.

Laika, a Russian dog, enjoyed a transient *fame when she became the first dog to go into space, but she was soon forgotten.*

triangle *n.* a polygon having three sides; also a love affair with three people involved.

A number of great novels and love poems are based upon a triangle *involving a man, his wife, and a lover.*

trudge *v.* to walk without spirit; to move with difficulty.

After trudging *through Hawaii's Volcano National Park, the hikers were quite happy to find a rest area at the top of the mountain.*

turmoil *n.* a state of complete confusion.

The bank robbers attempted to create turmoil *nearby as a diversion before robbing the bank.*

turpitude *n.* wickedness; depravity.

The theft of the widow's only automobile was an act of turpitude.

U

ubiquitous *adj.* widespread; being everywhere at the same time.

Most early civilizations have left evidence of widespread belief in a ubiquitous *deity that sees and knows everything.*

ultra *adj.* highest; extreme.

The space program reached ultra *heights with man's walk on the moon.*

umbilical cord *n.* a tethering or supporting line.

During man-made and natural disasters, the American Red Cross is an umbilical cord *to survival.*

umbrage *n.* a feeling of being easily offended.

President Truman, during his 1945–1953 administration, took umbrage *when the press criticized his daughter's singing and he retaliated by lashing out at the critics.*

unconscionable *adj.* not guided by conscience; lacking scruples or common values.

The young man's duplicity toward his parents was unconscionable *and could not be excused.*

unctuous *adj.* falsely earnest; smug.

Charles Dickens created unctuous *characters who were parodies of priggish Victorian people of the nineteenth century.*

unremitting *adj.* unrelenting; unyielding.

Her constant shopping excursions and unremitting *extravagance brought her and her family close to bankruptcy.*

unwitting *adj.* not intended; unaware.

She gave unwitting *encouragement to her rival when she cancelled the appointment.*

urbane *adj.* polished in manner; smooth; knowledgeable in social ways.

Ebony was one of the first major magazines to target the urbane *African American market.*

urge *v.* to insist on; to encourage or to press.

The judge gave his orders to the jury and ended by saying, "I urge *you to consider this question with all fairness and as expeditiously as possible."*

usurp *v.* to take over; to supplant.

Many factions have been trying to usurp *Tibet's Dalai Lama's traditional power.*

utopia *n.* an imaginary ideal place.

The sixteenth-century writer and statesman Sir Thomas More created the perfect political and social city when he wrote of Utopia.

utterance *n.* a brief, spoken communication.

The young woman eagerly responded to her fiance's every utterance.

V

vacillate *v.* to have difficulty choosing; to change positions.

Lyndon Johnson could not make up his mind and vacillated for several weeks before deciding against running for a second term as president.

vapid *adj.* dull; lacking interest.

Though considered vapid *and trite by many art critics, Norman Rockwell produced 300 covers for* The Saturday Evening Post.

venerate *v.* to honor; to serve with devotion.

The American public venerated *Franklin D. Roosevelt during World War II and mourned his death in 1945.*

verbosity *n.* wordiness; use of flamboyant language.

His effectiveness in his new position was threatened by his verbosity.

viable *adj.* capable of surviving; presumed possible.

The town council believed that the new plan for improving the traffic flow was a viable *one and they voted to accept it.*

vindicate *v.* to avenge; to get even.

Mothers Against Drunk Driving (MADD), a powerful organization, vindicates *mothers who have lost children in traffic accidents involving drunk drivers.*

virulent *adj.* extremely poisonous; malignant.

Tuberculosis, a virulent *bacteria that attacks the lungs and other organs, was once known as the white plague.*

vocation *n.* occupation.

Ellen was happy with her chosen vocation, *computer programming.*

void *v.* to cancel; to nullify.

Whenever you void *a check you have written, you should make sure that it is destroyed.*

W

wanton *adj.* lewd; coarse; unrestrained.

Nineteenth-century nurses were often pictured as lewd and wanton women.

willful *adj.* stubborn; disinclined to conform.

Willful young people may have difficulty adjusting to military life.

wistful *adj.* melancholy; sad.

The children appeared wistful when they learned that their teacher had been injured in a car accident.

X

xenophobe *n.* one who is unduly fearful or suspicious of foreign people.

Children who chant rhymes making fun of other children may have parents who are xenophobes.

Y

yearn *v.* to strongly desire something.

One of the myths of pregnancy was that a woman yearned for pickles when she was carrying a child.

yokel *n.* a gullible, innocent person from the country.

In early movies, the character of a yokel was often used as comic relief for the more sophisticated characters to ridicule.

Z

zany *adj.* crazy; acting to amuse others.

The clown, who was completely zany, broke up the audience with his antics.

zealous *adj.* possessing a fervor or zeal or passion.

Hoping for a winning season, the new coach wanted to recruit only the most zealous students for the soccer team.

APPENDIX A

WORD LIST CHART

Appendix A consists of a two-page Word List Chart for additional preparation for the GED test. Unlike the 400 words that are listed alphabetically, the following Word List Chart divides words into the special categories: direction words, writing skills, grammar, science, social studies, graphs, mathematics, and interpreting literature and the arts.

To make the best use of the chart, you may want to review the words under each category. If you feel confident about some words but uncertain about others, this is a good time to review the words that are still unclear.

Direction Words	Writing Skills	Grammar	Science
acceptable	allegory	adjective	absorb
accord	analogy	adverb	acid
analyze	body	clause	acidic
base	brainstorm	comma	alloy
compare	conclusion	compound	analyze
conclusion	dialogue	contraction	arc
contrast	essay	gerund	asexual
data	introduction	phrase	base
deduce	metaphor	punctuate	bile
defend	monologue	subject	binary
definitive	simile		component
denotation	structure		derivative
diagram	subject		desiccate
divide	support		dissolution
expository	thesis		ecology
introduction	topic		ecosystem
manifest			element
paradigm			emission
punctuate			erosion
query			fauna
rebut	.		fissure
subject			helix
syllogism			herbivore
thesis			hibernate
topic			high-energy
			latitude
			nocturnal
			nutrient

Social Studies	Graphs	Mathematics	Interpreting Literature and the Arts
abdicate	bar graph	adjacent	adapt
accord	base	arc	allegory
anarchy	diagram	axiom	analogy
appease		axis	anonymous
bill		bar graph	apocalypse
boondoggle		base	ballad
boycott		binary	biography
candidate		component	character
capitalism		compound	contemporary
communism		data	decadent
demagogue		decade	dialogue
democracy		divide	diction
dictator		divisible	didactic
disenfranchise		ellipse	disseminate
ecology		fraction	epigram
ecosystem		oblique	epilogue
equator		quadrangle	existential
filibuster		quadrant	figurative
herbivore		quintet	foreshadow
heresy		square	genre
hierarchy		triangle	hedonism
imperialism			ideology
juggernaut			idol
maritime			irony
monarchy			juxtapose
nepotism			
nihilism			

APPENDIX B

PRACTICE TESTS

TEST YOUR GED WORD POWER

Exercise 1

The following ten verbs can be found in the directions for the five GED tests. They have been selected from an actual GED Practice Test. Choose the best answer among the four possibilities, A, B, C, and D. Answers follow each exercise.

1. **describe**
   (A) repeat
   (B) depict
   (C) decry
   (D) sanction

2. **choose**
   (A) pick
   (B) base
   (C) check
   (D) maintain

3. **interpret**
   (A) make clear
   (B) flourish
   (C) accumulate
   (D) anticipate

4. **respond**
   (A) delude
   (B) rectify
   (C) reply
   (D) reiterate

5. **argue**
   (A) quarrel
   (B) plead
   (C) hasten
   (D) arrange

6. **construct**
   (A) separate
   (B) build
   (C) expand
   (D) verify

7. **support**
   (A) undergo
   (B) propose
   (C) signal
   (D) uphold

8. **convey**
   (A) express
   (B) pilfer
   (C) beckon
   (D) commence

9. **refer**
   (A) carry
   (B) rush
   (C) reinstate
   (D) attribute

10. **ascertain**
    (A) maintain
    (B) placate
    (C) determine
    (D) polarize

Answers—Exercise 1:

1. **B**		6. **B**	
2. **A**		7. **D**	
3. **A**		8. **A**	
4. **C**		9. **D**	
5. **B**		10. **C**	

Exercise 2

GED Test 1: Writing Skills measures your ability to use clear and effective English. The objective of this test is to show how English is written, not how it is spoken. The following practice vocabulary quiz reviews your understanding of words about writing skills. Choose the best synonym. Answers follow.

1. **thesis**
   (A) temperature
   (B) main idea
   (C) brainstorm
   (D) exercise

2. **topic**
   (A) extremity
   (B) fabric
   (C) subject
   (D) sensitivity

3. **structure**
   (A) façade
   (B) engage
   (C) rustle
   (D) plan

4. **conclusion**
   (A) command
   (B) brink
   (C) ending
   (D) absolution

5. **introduction**
   (A) prelude
   (B) condemnation
   (C) explanation
   (D) supposition

6. **body**
   (A) figure
   (B) main part
   (C) pinpoint
   (D) struggle

7. **outline**
   (A) stamp
   (B) artistic
   (C) form
   (D) end game

8. **organize**
   (A) believe
   (B) arrange
   (C) transfer
   (D) direct

9. **essay**
   (A) special
   (B) purpose
   (C) composition
   (D) recipe

10. **develop**
    (A) expand
    (B) destroy
    (C) command
    (D) general

Answers—Exercise 2:

1. **B**		6. **B**	
2. **C**		7. **C**	
3. **D**		8. **B**	
4. **C**		9. **C**	
5. **A**		10. **A**	

Exercise 3

GED Test 2: Social Studies consists of multiple-choice questions that often refer to maps, graphs, charts, cartoons, and/or figures. The following practice vocabulary quiz is based on words in GED Test 2. Select the best synonym. Answers follow.

1. **cause**
   (A) purpose
   (B) reason
   (C) casual
   (D) mitigation

2. **status**
   (A) strident
   (B) makeshift
   (C) sensation
   (D) position

3. **distribution**
   (A) district
   (B) allocation
   (C) interception
   (D) quantity

4. **emphasis**
   (A) instinct
   (B) immediate
   (C) stress
   (D) dissertation

5. **compares**
   (A) likens
   (B) reduces
   (C) entitles
   (D) strives

6. **valid**
   (A) opposition
   (B) sound
   (C) distinct
   (D) appreciably

7. **graph**
   (A) container
   (B) solace
   (C) chart
   (D) proscription

8. **evidence**
   (A) heading
   (B) makeshift
   (C) plausible
   (D) proof

9. **control**
   (A) regulate
   (B) haunt
   (C) motion
   (D) provide

10. **empty**
    (A) harness
    (B) provide
    (C) bring about
    (D) vacate

Answers—Exercise 3:

1. **B**		6. **B**
2. **D**		7. **C**
3. **B**		8. **D**
4. **C**		9. **A**
5. **A**		10. **D**

Exercise 4

Words associated with science constitute a large part of our vocabulary. The following ten words are often used in science. They may appear in GED Test 3. Select the word closest in meaning. Answers follow.

1. **mass**
   (A) bulk
   (B) round
   (C) length
   (D) size

4. **intensity**
   (A) precipitous
   (B) rugged
   (C) informal
   (D) strong effect

2. **factor**
   (A) harmony
   (B) path
   (C) divisor
   (D) amount

5. **orbit**
   (A) circular path
   (B) map
   (C) minion
   (D) alignment

3. **aquatic**
   (A) umbrage
   (B) on or in water
   (C) agile
   (D) blue-green

6. **generate**
   (A) handle
   (B) reproduce
   (C) portray
   (D) act

7. **vapor**
   (A) vacant
   (B) pleasure
   (C) gaseous state
   (D) halo

8. **vacuum**
   (A) empty space
   (B) hideout
   (C) cove
   (D) site

9. **pure**
   (A) link
   (B) unadulterated
   (C) masked
   (D) depleted

10. **dormant**
    (A) obvious
    (B) active
    (C) noisy
    (D) latent

Answers—Exercise 4:

1. **A**		6. **B**
2. **C**		7. **C**
3. **B**		8. **A**
4. **D**		9. **B**
5. **A**		10. **D**

Exercise 5

GED Test 4: Interpreting Literature and the Arts consists of excerpts from both the classics and today's popular art forms. Here are ten words frequently used in this test that are particularly related to reading comprehension. Choose the word closest in meaning. Answers follow.

1. **narrator**
   (A) salesman
   (B) manager
   (C) storyteller
   (D) accountant

2. **universal**
   (A) exceptional
   (B) exclusive
   (C) far-reaching
   (D) makeshift

3. **implied**
   (A) specific
   (B) inferred
   (C) obvious
   (D) fictional

4. **contrast**
   (A) difference
   (B) solution
   (C) light
   (D) exponential

5. **excerpt**
   (A) volume
   (B) journey
   (C) part
   (D) difficultly

6. **ridicule**
   (A) praise
   (B) relate
   (C) pose
   (D) mock

7. **relationship**
   (A) connection
   (B) inkling
   (C) memorable
   (D) forecast

8. **similar**
   (A) loud
   (B) alike
   (C) style
   (D) link

9. **image**
   (A) sensory impression
   (B) information
   (C) ability
   (D) particle

10. **criticism**
    (A) decorative
    (B) evaluation
    (C) notation
    (D) progressive

Answers—Exercise 5:

1. **C**		6. **D**	
2. **C**		7. **A**	
3. **B**		8. **B**	
4. **A**		9. **A**	
5. **C**		10. **B**	

Exercise 6

In Test 5: Mathematics, the following ten words are frequently used to describe, explain, or question a student about mathematics. Select the word nearest in meaning from the following list. Answers follow.

1. **formulate**
   (A) guess
   (B) speculate
   (C) major
   (D) develop

2. **gain**
   (A) harden
   (B) gradually increase
   (C) detain
   (D) mount

3. **rate**
   (A) standard scale
   (B) crossover
   (C) moderate
   (D) positive

4. **represent**
   (A) relate
   (B) speak for
   (C) analyze
   (D) migrate

5. **scale**
   (A) measure
   (B) simplify
   (C) retain
   (D) dispose

6. **add**
   (A) take away
   (B) enlarge
   (C) place
   (D) amortize

7. **base**
   (A) annoy
   (B) tape
   (C) indulge
   (D) establish

8. **measure**
   (A) violate
   (B) determine
   (C) censor
   (D) picture

APPENDIX B

9. **compute**
   (A) manage
   (B) place
   (C) circulate
   (D) count

10. **record**
    (A) explore
    (B) simulate
    (C) make an entry
    (D) place

Answers—Exercise 6:

1.	**D**	6.	**B**
2.	**B**	7.	**D**
3.	**A**	8.	**B**
4.	**B**	9.	**D**
5.	**A**	10.	**C**

SOURCES

American Council on Education. *The Tests of General Educational Development Technical Manual,* 1st ed. Washington, D.C.: GED Testing Service, 1993.

American Council on Education. *Who Took the GED? GED 1996 Statistical Report,* The Center for Adult Learning and Educational Credentials. Washington, D.C.: GED Testing Service, 1996.

Merriam Webster's Collegiate Dictionary, 10th ed. Springfield, MA.: Merriam-Webster, Inc.,1994.

The New Roget's Thesaurus in Dictionary Form. New York: The Berkley Book Publishing Group, 1986.

Legett, Glenn, C. David Meand, and Melinda G. Kramer. *Prentice Hall Handbook for Writers,* 11th ed. Englewood Cliffs, NJ: Prentice Hall, 1991.